Valentine's Day

Written by Ireta Sitts Graube

Illustrated by Theresa M. Wright

Teacher Created Materials, Inc.

P.O. Box 1040

Huntington Beach, CA 92647

©1992 Teacher Created Materials, Inc.

Made in U.S.A.

ISBN 1-55734-260-1

Table of Contents

Introduction

Valentine's Day contains a captivating whole language, thematic unit. Its 80 exciting pages are filled with a wide variety of lesson ideas and activities designed for use with primary children. At its core are two high-quality children's literature selections, *The Valentine Bears* and *One Zillion Valentines*, and an original, reproducible book, *My Heart Book.* For each of these books, activities are included which set the stage for reading, encourage the enjoyment of the book, and extend the concepts gained. In addition, the theme is connected to the curriculum with activities in language arts (including daily writing suggestions), math, science, social studies, art, music, and life skills. Many of these activities encourage cooperative learning. Furthermore, directions for student-created Big Books and culminating activities, which allow students to synthesize their knowledge in order to produce products that can be shared beyond the classroom, highlight this very complete teacher resource.

This thematic unit includes:

❑ **literature selections**—summaries of two children's books and an original, nonfiction manuscript with related lessons (complete with reproducible pages) that cross the curriculum

❑ **poetry**—suggested selections and lessons enabling students to write and publish their own works

❑ **planning guides**—suggestions for sequencing lessons each day of the unit

❑ **writing and language experience ideas**—daily suggestions as well as writing activities across the curriculum, including Big Books

❑ **bulletin board ideas**—suggestions for student-created and/or interactive bulletin boards

❑ **homework suggestions**—extending the unit to the child's home

❑ **curriculum connections**—in language arts, math, science, social studies, art, music, and life skills

❑ **group projects**—to foster cooperative learning

❑ **a culminating activity**—which requires students to synthesize their learning to produce a product or engage in an activity that can be shared with others

❑ **a bibliography**—suggesting additional literature and nonfiction books on the theme

---

To keep this valuable resource intact so that it can be used year after year, you may wish to punch holes in the pages and store them in a three-ring binder.

Introduction *(cont.)*

Why Whole Language?

A whole language approach involves children in using all modes of communication: reading, writing, listening, observing, illustrating, experiencing, and doing. Communication skills are interconnected and integrated into lessons that emphasize the whole of language rather than isolating its parts. The lessons revolve around selected literature. Reading is not taught as a separate subject from writing and spelling, for example. A child reads, writes (spelling appropriately for his/her level), speaks, listens, etc. in response to a literature experience introduced by the teacher. In this way, language skills grow naturally, stimulated by involvement and interest in the topic at hand.

Why Thematic Planning?

One very useful tool for implementing an integrated whole language program is thematic planning. By choosing a theme with correlating literature selections for a unit of study, a teacher can plan activities throughout the day that lead to a cohesive, in-depth study of the topic. Students will be practicing and applying their skills in meaningful contexts. Consequently, they will tend to learn and retain more. Both teachers and students will be freed from a day that is broken into unrelated segments of isolated drill and practice.

Why Cooperative Learning?

Besides academic skills and content, students need to learn social skills. No longer can this area of development be taken for granted. Students must learn to work cooperatively in groups in order to function well in modern society. Group activities should be a regular part of school life and teachers should consciously include social objectives as well as academic objectives in their planning. For example, a group working together to write a report may need to select a leader. The teacher should make clear to the students and monitor the qualities of good leader-following group interaction just as he/she would state and monitor the academic goals of the project.

Why Big Books?

An excellent cooperative, whole language activity is the production of Big Books. Groups of students, or the whole class, can apply their language skills, content knowledge, and creativity to produce a Big Book that can become a part of the classroom library to be read and reread. These books make excellent culminating projects for sharing beyond the classroom with parents, librarians, other classes, etc. Big Books can be produced in many ways and this thematic unit book includes directions for at least one method you may choose.

History of Valentine's Day

No one is certain how Valentine's Day first started. There are several different theories. The first theory took place in Roman times, about 2,700 years ago. Rome is a city in Italy and when it was built, hungry wolves surrounded its city walls and howled at night. They ate the people's sheep and sometimes even killed people. The Romans were afraid of the wolves, so they prayed to one of their gods Lupercus (Loo-PER-kus), to protect them. Lupercus was the Roman god who watched over sheep and shepherds. They prayed to this god on a special holiday named Lupercalia (Loo-per-Kay-lee-ah). This holiday was held on February 15th each year. Even after the wolves had disappeared, the Romans kept celebrating the holiday because they enjoyed it. But as the years passed, Lupercus became less important to the people and they started celebrating a holiday for Juno instead. Juno was the queen of the Roman gods. She ruled over marriage. This was a holiday for love. On this day, young Roman women wrote their names on pieces of paper and placed them in a bowl. Young men drew out the names on February 14th, and the names they drew would be their partners for dances and games on this holiday.

Another theory suggests that when the Christian church became powerful in Roman times, the Christians didn't want the Romans celebrating holidays for their old gods, so they made the old customs into Christian holidays. The Christians found a saint to honor named Valentine. St. Valentine secretly married people because the Roman Emperor, Claudius, had ruled that no men could marry because he wanted soldiers in his armies. Claudius also knew married men would want to stay home with their families. When Emperor Claudius found out about the secret marriages, he had St. Valentine thrown in jail and later beheaded on February 14th.

There is another story about a man named Valentine. This man had also helped Christians. Emperor Claudius did not like Christians so he had this man jailed, too. While this man was in jail he met the jailer's daughter. She was blind and Valentine performed a miracle that cured the girl's blindness. This made Claudius angry, so he ordered this man put to death on February 14. Before Valentine died, he sent a poem to the little girl signed, "From your Valentine."

Still another possible origin for Valentine's Day took place in Europe hundreds of years ago. People noticed that some birds chose their mates around February 14th. Since birds did this, they thought people should, too. Today we see birds used on valentine cards. They stand for the times when people believed that birds chose their mates for life around Valentine's Day. Today we call two people who are very happy together "lovebirds."

History of Valentine's Day
(cont.)

No one knows if these stories are really true or which of these theories is the one that brought us Valentine's Day. But we do know that we celebrate Saint Valentine's Day on February 14th, and it was brought to us in the new world by the pilgrims many years ago.

Have you ever wondered why we use the heart shape on valentines? Heart shapes are used on valentines because, many years ago, people believed that the heart was the center of our feelings. We now know that the brain is the center, but we still use the old sayings to indicate our heart has feelings. Have you ever said, "He broke my heart" or "It does my heart good to hear that story"? Before we knew what the heart was actually shaped like, we thought it looked like the heart we see on valentines today.

We sometimes see Cupid on valentines. He evolved from the Greek god called Eros (Ir'os), the god of love. Cupid is a chubby little baby with wings and curly hair. He usually shoots an arrow into people's hearts. This arrow does not hurt them, but makes them fall in love with someone.

Ribbons on valentines go back to the knights on horseback. Women would give a little piece of ribbon to a knight when he went to war. He would carry this ribbon to remind him of his love.

Roses and flowers are often seen on valentines. The rose is known as the flower of love. Violets and bachelor's buttons are also seen on valentine cards. One story says that Saint Valentine sent notes on violets from his jail cell. The birds carried the notes to people.

Lace is often used on valentines. It comes from the Latin language and means "to catch." If you put lace on your valentine, you are supposed to catch the heart of the person you give it to.

In England and France, people send valentines only to their sweethearts. They do not usually sign their names on the cards. The person who gets the card may never know who sent it. But, in the United States, we give valentines to family and friends.

The Valentine Bears

by Eve Bunting

Summary

Mrs. Bear decides she wants to celebrate Valentine's Day with Mr. Bear, so she sets her alarm to go off on February 14th. Mr. Bear sleeps on as she makes signs, digs up honey, and makes a berry mix. She tries to wake Mr. Bear, but he is not interested in getting up. What happens next is a fun, warm-hearted story of two bears enjoying themselves on Valentine's Day.

The outline below is a suggested plan for using the various activities that are presented in this unit. You should adapt these ideas to fit your own classroom situations.

Sample Plan

Day 1

- Get centers ready. See Overview of Activities on page 8.
- Show the cover of *The Valentine Bears* and discuss.
- Read part of the book. See page 9 for details.
- Write bear poetry. (page 12)
- Work Valentine Math Puzzles. (page 13)
- Decorate and send home invitations to Bear Valentine Party.
- Learn the song and game "You Are Mine." (page 69)

Day 2

- Introduce song "I Am Making Valentines." (page 70)
- Weave a Bear's Valentine Heart (page 14); sing the song as you work.
- Make a pie graph on the playground. (page 57)
- Make notes for Fortune Cookies. (page 74)
- Play "You Are Mine" again. (page 69)

Day 3

- Work the Crossword Puzzle. (page 51)
- Introduce the Block Bar Graph. (page 16)
- Paint paper plate red for Picture Heart. (page 14)
- Make Fortune Cookies for Bear Party. (page 74)
- Make Bear name tags for dramatization. (page 73)
- Sing "I Am Making Valentines" (pages 70) and introduce Valentine chanting. (page 67)

Day 4

- Complete Hearts in Order. (page 55)
- Have a preview of plays for the Bear Party. (page 73)
- Make Paper Plate Picture Valentines using red plates. (page 14)
- Make Bears and Honey Roll-Up Treats. (page 17)

Day 5

- Make Red Punch for guests. (page 74)
- Make a Valentine Window House. (page 15)
- Have the Valentines Bear Party with guests and parents. (page 73)

Overview of Activities

SETTING THE STAGE

1. Collect books about bears for the reading center. See the learning center ideas on page 10 for ideas about starting bear centers.

2. Get ready to start a traveling class bear. Purchase a teddy bear, use one you already have, or ask for a donation from your students. (Garage sales often have inexpensive stuffed animals, if you need to buy one.) Make a cloth or plastic bag or use a suitcase to store the bear. Collect or make clothing that will fit the bear and/or a small comb and brush and toothbrush for the bear. Send home the letter on page 76 to inform parents that the bear will be visiting. Include this same letter in the bear bag, in case parents forget what is happening with this bear. Include a notebook in the bag and encourage children and/or parents to tell about the bear's adventures at their home. See page 11 for a cover for your bear notebook. Introduce the bear to the class and let them vote on a name for this class bear. Explain that the bear will be going home with them overnight and tell them about the notebook. Send the bear home with the children on an overnight check-out basis. When each child brings the bear back to class, read aloud from the notebook the bear's adventures with that child's family.

3. Collect stuffed bears for a special bear display. Ask the children to bring their favorite bear from home. Provide a table for display. Provide note cards, pencils, and crayons so children can write the names of their bears or their own names on cards and place them next to their bears. Or if they would like to make necklace note cards, provide yarn or string, a hole punch, and scissors so they can hang the names on the teddy bears.

8

Overview of Activities *(cont.)*

ENJOYING THE BOOK

1. Show the cover of *The Valentine Bears*. What do the children think will happen in this book? List their ideas on a chart and save for later discussion.

2. Read *The Valentine Bears* up to the part where Mrs. Bear gets a can of ice water and is counting. Ask the children to predict what will happen next. Discuss.

3. Finish reading the book. Discuss fact and fiction. Which is this book? Why? Discuss the children's predictions from the chart that you made earlier.

4. Make necklace name tags and act out the story of Mr. and Mrs. Bear. See page 73 for directions.

5. Buy or ask parents for donations of honey and graham crackers. Serve this treat. If possible get different types of honey and let the children sample each kind. See if they can tell the difference.

6. Write a language experience story about Mr. and Mrs. Bear. How do the children think the bears feel at the beginning of the story and at the end? What would it be like to live in a cave? Would humans be cold in the winter? Why aren't bears cold in the winter?

EXTENDING THE BOOK

1. The tasting of honey might lead to a discussion of bees and how honey is made. Get books from the library on bees. Read and discuss.

2. Make Bears and Honey Roll-Ups. See page 17 for directions.

3. Make a web or chart on butcher paper with questions about bears. Let the children ask questions as you write them on the web. Keep this chart visible as you study bears. When the children discover an answer, write it on the chart.

4. Begin a study of real bears. See the bibliography for suggestions of books.

5. Let the children write down bear facts or copy them from the web. Each child will write and illustrate one or two facts on a sheet of paper. These papers can be placed on a bulletin board or compiled into a class bear book.

Learning Centers

Reading Center

Whether you are teaching the unit about Valentine's Day, bears, or hearts, assemble books on that subject at a reading center. Ask the children to bring books and tapes from home on the subjects. Be sure they put their names on all items. Visit your school and local library, and ask other teachers for books on the theme.

If you have an extra desk, table, or book shelf, display the books you have gathered. Make this area as comfortable as possible. Use cushions, rocking chairs, rugs, etc. The children will love coming here to read the new books.

Art Center

Base this center at a table or desk. Supply paper, glue, tape, scissors, stapler, paints, markers, crayons, and patterns for the children to use to make valentines, hearts, or bears. Have a bear (page 11) and valentine pattern (page 13) for children to trace around and decorate. If you are working on a heart unit, supply rolls of butcher paper for tracing around the body. (page 41)

Writing Center

Have empty books assembled in which the children may write their stories. Also, sheets of lined and unlined paper for illustrations and sentences should be supplied. Crayons, markers, glue, construction paper, scissors, tape, and pencils should also be at this center. Have this center near a bulletin board. Children can put their story or book up on the bulletin board with a push pin when they are done writing it. If they need several days to complete their writing, supply a box or basket for them to store their books in until they are completed.

Science Center

For the bear unit, this center could contain items a bear might eat, i.e. dried berries and fruit, bark, twigs. If a bear skin is available or an article of clothing made from bear hide, display this at the center. Or show samples of different types of fur from animals.

When you are ready to study the heart unit, supply the items on pages 59-60 for children to experiment with.

Bear Pattern

Use this pattern at
learning centers, as a
journal cover, or to
make invitations.

Poetry

Directions: In *The Valentine Bears*, Mrs. Bear wrote two poems to give to Mr Bear. She could not decide which poem she liked the best.

"Red Berries are red
Blue Berries are blue,
Termites are sweet,
And you are, too."

or

"Your teeth are so sharp,
Your claws are so fine,
Dear Mr. Bear,
You are my Valentine."

If we examine these poems we can see which verses rhyme in each poem. Underline the words that rhyme in each poem.

Try making up poetry for the bears or for your family that have the second and fourth lines rhyming. For example:

Valentines are red,
They never are blue,
Candy is sweet,
And you are, too.

A valentine for you,
My very best teacher,
It is all I have
For such a fine creature.

Write your poems on valentine cards. See page 14.

12

Valentine Math Puzzles

Materials: red construction paper; pattern below; 9" x 6" (23 cm x 15 cm) envelopes; laminator or contact paper; scissors; marker

Teacher Preparation: Use the pattern below to trace on red construction paper. You may wish to enlarge the pattern. Write a number or an equation on the front of the valentine and write the answer to the equation on the back. Cut the valentine into three parts. Laminate the parts and place them in a bag or manila folder. Repeat this procedure for each puzzle, but cut each one in a different pattern.

Directions: Give the children the bags and let them solve the puzzles. Children love solving these puzzles and discovering the answers to the problems.

Extensions:

1. Write vocabulary words, antonyms, synonyms, rhyming words, etc. on the valentines.

2. Make copies of the valentine pattern and let children make their own puzzles for each other. They can put any math or reading work on the puzzle.

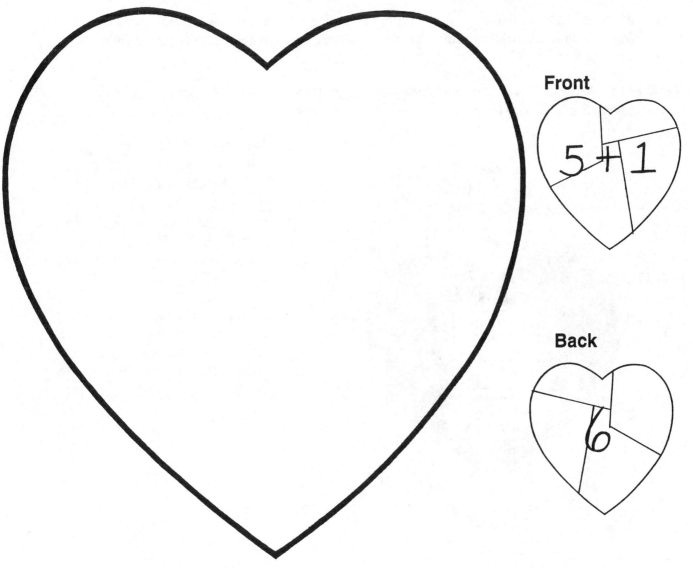

Front

Back

Bear's Valentine Heart

Materials: 9" x 11" (23 cm x 30 cm) red construction paper; hole punch; white or pink yarn or ribbon; newspaper; crayons, colored pencils or paints

Directions: Make two red hearts by tracing the heart pattern (page 13) on red construction paper. Cut out. Punch holes around all edges of the valentine about ¹/₂" (1.3 cm) from the side. Thread the yarn or ribbon through the holes and tie it in a bow. (If the yarn is difficult to thread through the holes, wrap a piece of clear tape around the end.) Copy one of the poems you wrote (page 12) onto the front of the valentine. Decorate with crayons, colored pencils, or paints.

Paper Plate Picture Heart

If Mrs. Bear had a paper plate and a picture, she could have made this special valentine for Mr. Bear.

Materials: pink, white, or red crepe paper; paper plate; picture of someone you want to send a valentine to or a picture of yourself; white construction paper; glue; clear tape; red paint; string or yarn; hole punch; scissors; markers

Teacher Preparation: Cut the crepe paper from a roll in 2" (5 cm) strips. The strips should be approximately 5-6' (1¹/₂-2m) long.

Directions: Paint the paper plate red. Let it dry. Draw a large heart on it and cut it out. Glue the picture in the center of the heart. Write your message on a piece of paper and glue it on the plate. Stretch one edge of the crepe paper and bunch the other edge around the heart plate.

Glue the crepe paper to the edge of the heart, creating a ruffle. Make a small hole in the top with the hole punch. Put yarn or string through the hole to hang your special valentine.

Valentine Window House

Materials: pattern; scissors; pencil; crayons; glue; 9" x 11" (23 cm x 30 cm) plain white paper

Directions: Cut out the sides of the house. Cut out the windows on the dotted line, leaving the solid line uncut so the windows and doors will open and close. This cutting can be done by pinching the paper slightly so you can make a cut with the scissors to get inside the paper and cut out the windows and doors. Using another sheet of plain paper, glue it to the house at the edges only. Cut off the edges so that it matches the house size. On each window and the door write a word. Inside that window or door, write a word that rhymes with that word. For example, write "love" on the door and "dove" on the inside of the door. Other activities using the house include: writing even numbers on the outside and odd numbers on the inside, or an equation on the outside and the answer on the inside. Use the house to make the bulletin board on page 75.

A Valentine Block Bar Graph

Materials: one block or interlocking cube per child (the blocks need to all be the same size), three 3" x 5" (8 cm x 13 cm) notecards, three different sizes of red valentines, red construction paper, (patterns below), scissors, pencil or pen

Teacher Preparation:

1. Using the patterns below, cut one construction paper valentine for each child in the class. Cut enough valentines so that half of the class will get a big one and the rest will get a medium size or small one.

2. Cut three more valentines and glue them on folded notecards. Place these cards on the table or the floor so the children can place their blocks beside the appropriate card.

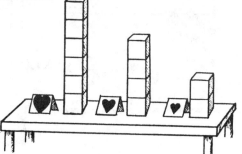

Directions: Each child will receive one valentine. They will need to place their block by the appropriate notecard, stacking one block on top of the other. Explain that this looks like a bar graph. How many blocks are in the tallest pile? Which size valentine has the least? The most?

Bears and Honey Roll-Ups

Ingredients: peanut butter, whole wheat bread, honey for drizzling, table knives, one sharp knife, rolling pin, round toothpicks, wax paper

Directions: You will need one slice of bread for every two children. The children will work in partners making one roll-up for each pair.

Variations: Use jelly, jam, or cream cheese. Try cinnamon instead of honey.

Make a copy of this recipe for the children to take home and make with their families.

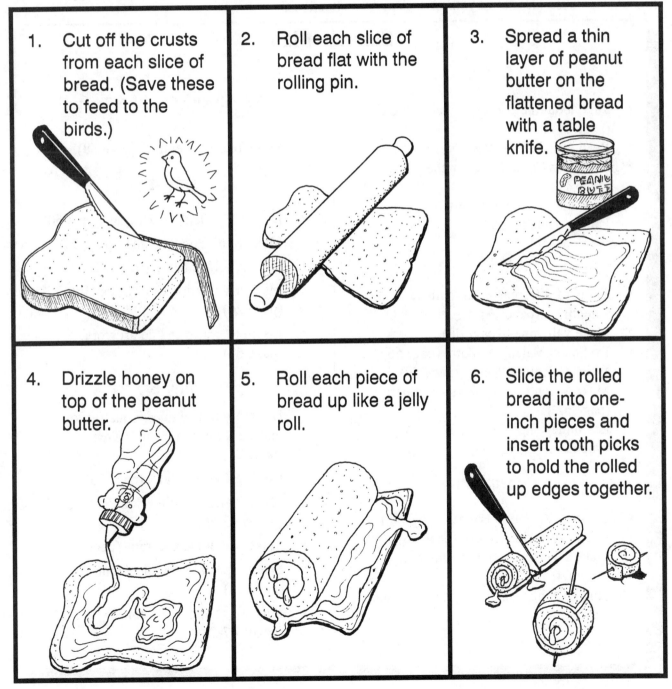

1. Cut off the crusts from each slice of bread. (Save these to feed to the birds.)

2. Roll each slice of bread flat with the rolling pin.

3. Spread a thin layer of peanut butter on the flattened bread with a table knife.

4. Drizzle honey on top of the peanut butter.

5. Roll each piece of bread up like a jelly roll.

6. Slice the rolled bread into one-inch pieces and insert tooth picks to hold the rolled up edges together.

One Zillion Valentines

by Frank Modell

Summary

Valentine's Day is one of Marvin's favorite days, but his friend, Milton, is less than enthusiastic about it. To get Milton into the spirit of Valentine's Day, Marvin shows him how to make valentines and together they make enough for everyone in the neighborhood. After delivering the valentines, they enterprisingly sell the remaining cards and buy a Valentine treat for themselves.

The outline below is a suggested plan for using the various activities that are presented in this unit. You should adapt these ideas to fit your own classroom situations.

Sample Plan

Day 1

- Talk about the concept of one zillion. (page 19)
- Read *One Zillion Valentines*.
- Discuss what happened in the book. (page 19)
- Send home the questionnaire for the Family Tree. (page 25)

Day 2

- Think of different ways to make valentines. (page 19)
- Make valentines. (page 20)
- Do Secret Valentine Math. (page 53)
- Write Valentine Poetry. (page 50)
- Make Valentine Checkers and Board. (page 62)
- Learn the song "Do You Know My Valentine?" (page 68)

Day 3

- Create a Valentine Banner. (page 52)
- Count Valentine Hearts. (page 56)
- Make a This is Your Life valentine. (page 64)
- Sing all songs learned in the Valentine's Day unit.

- Make Valentine Chocolate Treats. (page 71)
- Play Freeze Valentine. (page 68)

Day 4

- Do some Valentine Writing. (page 50)
- Make Math Potato Prints. (page 54)
- Make a folded heart. (page 22)
- Make a Valentine Craft Stick Gift. (page 26)
- Listen to music and do art work. (page 67)

Day 5

- Use the returned questionnaires to make a Valentine Family Tree. (page 24)
- Do Egg Carton Math. (page 23)
- Make Valentine Pin Prick Pictures. (pages 65-66)
- Make Valentine Clusters. (page 27)
- Send a special valentine home. (page 20)
- Sing songs and play games. (pages 67-70)

Overview of Activities

SETTING THE STAGE

1. Prepare your classroom for Valentine's Day. Set up the learning centers and displays described on page 10.

2. Send home a letter explaining that the students will be hearing a story about two boys who make a zillion handmade valentines. Ask the parents to encourage their children to make handmade valentines for their classmates, instead of purchasing them at the store. Attach a class list (page 78) to the letter. Also ask parents to send in books about Valentine's Day for their child to share with the class.

ENJOYING THE BOOK

1. Show the cover and read the title of *One Zillion Valentines*. Ask the children if they think that is a lot of valentines? How many is that?

2. Read *One Zillion Valentines* to the children.

3. Discuss what happened in the book. Why do you think Marvin likes Valentine's Day so much? Why did Milton not like Valentine's Day? What did Marvin show Milton how to do? What did they do for Valentine's Day?

4. Take a survey of who likes Valentine's Day and who does not. Ask the children why they like or dislike Valentine's Day. Record their reasons on a large heart cut from butcher paper.

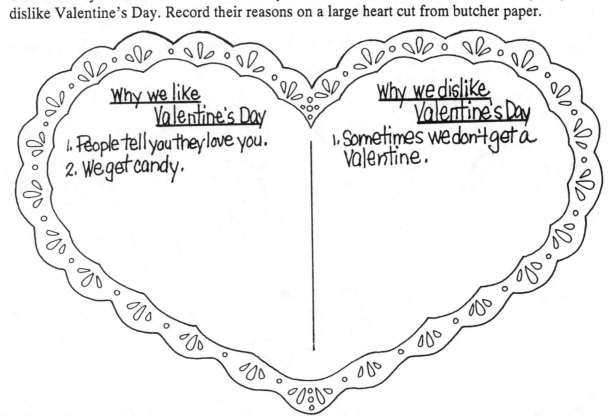

5. Talk about how Marvin and Milton made valentines. What are some other ways to make valentines?

Overview of Activities *(cont.)*

ENJOYING THE BOOK *(cont.)*

6. Supply different colors of construction paper, tape, staplers, scissors, watercolor paints, cotton balls, markers, and patterns for children to use to make a "zillion" valentines. Show them how to make a heart (page 22). Deliver the valentine's to school personnel, neighbors, or to a retirement home.

7. Have the students make a valentine for someone at home. Supply or make envelopes (page 21) to send the valentines in. Teach the children how to address envelopes. Each child can address an envelope to someone at home. This also reinforces learning addresses. Have the children draw a stamp on the envelope and hand deliver it to the intended receiver.

8. Have each child make a valentine pocket. Fold a 12" x 18" (31 cm x 46 cm) piece of red, pink, or white construction paper in half. Tape or staple the two sides together, leaving the top open. Decorate the pocket for Valentine's Day. On Valentine's Day they can deliver their valentines to each other's pockets.

EXTENDING THE BOOK

1. Read several books about valentines. See the bibliography on page 80 for suggestions.

2. Ask the children to tell their own stories about Valentine's Day. Encourage them to use their imaginations and to be descriptive. Remind students that a story should have a setting, a problem, and a solution. Have them write or dictate their stories so they can be bound into a class book of Valentine's Day stories.

3. Read the history of Valentine's Day on pages 5-6. Discuss the different items we use on Valentine's Day and their origins.

4. Have the students teach younger children how to make valentines.

5. Let the children write or dictate directions for something they like to do. Then have someone try to follow their directions. Talk about how important it is to give good directions and to follow them.

Make an Envelope

1. Cut out the pattern along the solid lines.

2. Put the pattern facedown on the table.

3. Fold in side flaps A and B. Put a little glue along the bottom edges where it says "glue."

4. Fold up flap C and glue it down.

5. Fold down flap D.

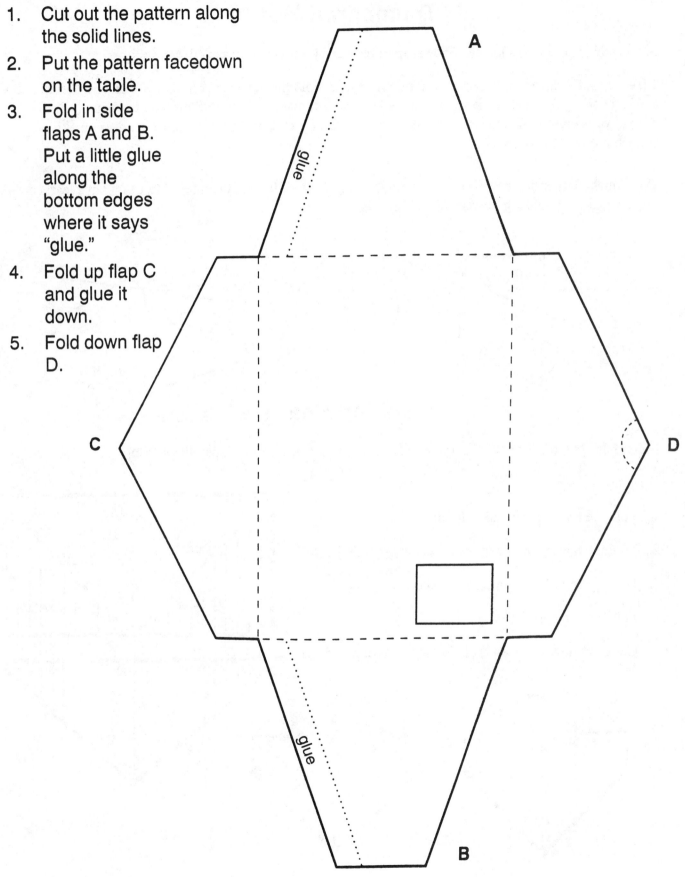

Making Hearts

Thumbprint Hearts

Materials: 6" (15 cm) squares of newspaper; red construction paper; pencil; scissors

Directions: Practice making hearts out of newspaper. Fold the newspaper in half. Place your left thumb at a slant along the folded edge. (If you are left handed, place your right thumb on the paper.) Trace around your thumb. Cut this out to make a heart. After you learn how to make a heart, try making some out of construction paper.

Try to make larger hearts by drawing around your hand with fingers together. After you have learned to make a heart, try making hearts with ruffled edges.

Folded Hearts

Materials: 3" x 6" (8 cm x 15 cm) rectangle of colored construction paper and scissors

Directions:

1. Fold the rectangle in half. Unfold it.

2. Fold the lower corners to the crease in the middle.

3. Fold the top corners into the middle.

4. Fold the top corners down.

5. Cut a ¼" down the center. Fold the flaps formed down.

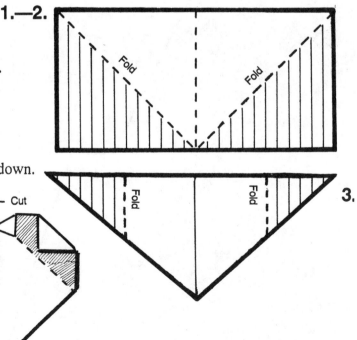

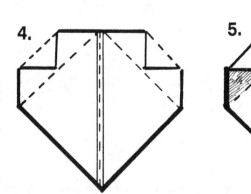

Egg Carton Math

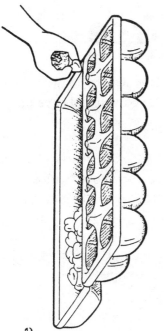

Materials: egg cartons; black permanent marker; candy hearts (2-3 bags); scissors; glue or tape

Teacher Preparation: Write numbers or equations in the bottom of each egg cup, such as 2+3=, or for children needing counting skills, just write a number in the bottom of the egg carton. Cut out the egg carton cover and glue it to the top of the carton.

Directions: Give each child an open egg carton with some candy hearts in the lid. They will need to solve the problems or count and place the correct number of hearts in each egg cup. You may wish to write the directions on this cover. Let them eat the answers when they're done with the problems!

Variations:

1. Let the children work with partners and solve the problems together.

2. For more advanced students, supply empty egg cartons. Let them write their own problems in the bottom of the carton. Trade with another partner to solve.

3. This game can be used for letter recognition, too. Write a letter in the bottom of each egg cup. Have the children look at each candy heart. If the message on the heart has one of the letters in an egg cup, they can drop it in. Ask them to name the letter as they put it in the carton.

Egg Carton Cover

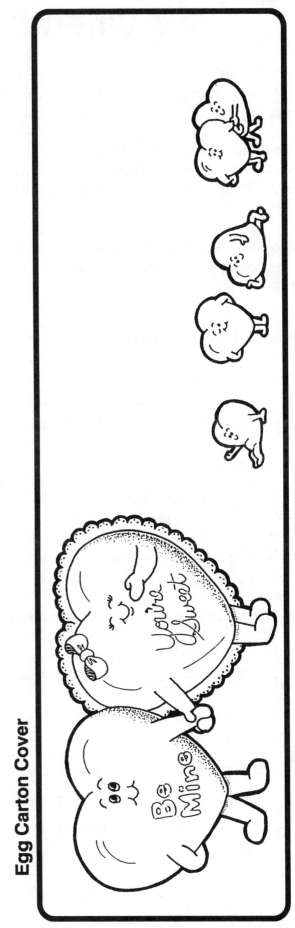

My Valentine Family Tree

On Valentine's Day we show our family members how much we love them. One way to do this might be to make a family tree and trace back the names of all the people who have loved you and have been loved by you.

Teacher Preparation: Make copies of the questionnaire on page 25 and send a copy home with each child. When these questionnaires are returned you are ready to start this project.

Materials: one piece of poster board, railroad board, oaktag or heavy paper per child; craft sticks; glue; thin-lined markers or pens; red construction paper; colored markers or crayons; completed questionnaires

Directions: Tell the children that they are going to make a Valentine family tree.

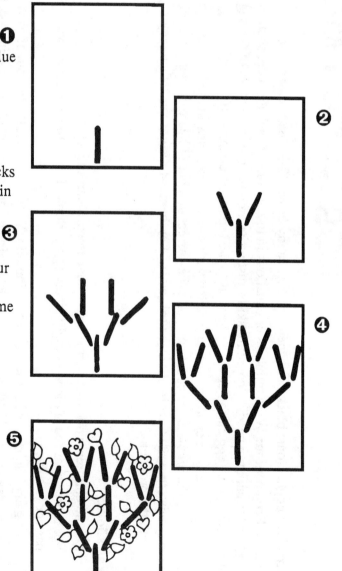

1. Write your first and last name on a craft stick. Glue this stick to the poster board to make the trunk of the tree.

2. Write your mother's maiden name and your father's name on two other sticks. Glue these sticks above the stick with your name on it. Glue them in the shape of a "Y" to make the branches.

3. Write the names of your mother's parents and your father's parents on four more sticks. Glue your mother's parents' names above your mother's name in a "Y" shape. Do the same with your father's parents above your father's name.

4. Do the same with your parents' grandparents. How many branches does your tree have?

5. Add leaves, hearts, and flowers if you would like.

Valentine Family Tree Questionnaire

Parents, could you please help your child fill out this questionnaire about your family. We are making a Valentine Family Tree. Please return this questionnaire by _____. Thank you.

Mother's Side	Father's Side
Mother's Full Name *(Include maiden name)*	**Father's Full Name**
Grandmother's Full Name *(Include maiden name)*	**Grandmother's Full Name** *(Include maiden name)*
Grandfather's Full Name	**Grandfather's Full Name**
Great-Grandmother's Full Name *(Include maiden name)*	**Great-Grandmother's Full Name** *(Include maiden name)*
Great-Grandfather's Full Name	**Great-Grandfather's Full Name**

Valentine Gifts

Materials: craft sticks; red construction paper; clear tape; stapler; marking pens

Directions: Trace the patterns below on red construction paper. Write a message on both sides of the heart. You might want to make part of a message on one side and complete the message on the other side.

Tape the hearts to the craft stick or staple them in place at the top of the stick. These little heart messages can be stuck in planters as gifts or sent to your favorite person.

Variations: Have students draw names of other students and make a stick heart for that person. Write that person's name on the stick. On the heart write a note to that person giving them some clue as to who it is from; e.g. "I have long brown hair." They do not sign their own name. Hide it somewhere in the classroom. As the children find their own stick hearts, they will have to guess who sent them by reading the clues.

Valentine Clusters

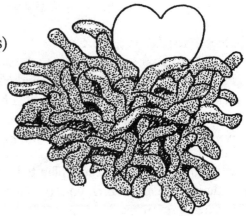

Ingredients:

1 package semi-sweet chocolate chips (12 oz./360g or 1 ½ cups)
½ cup (125 mL) chunky style peanut butter
4 cups chow mein noodles (6 oz./180g bag)
candy valentine hearts
You will also need one large glass bowl or metal pan; wax
paper; mixing spoons or large forks; two cookie trays or flat
pans to put cookies on; a microwave, oven, or hot plate.

Directions:

1. Put the chocolate chips and the peanut butter into a large glass or microwave bowl. Set the timer for one minute and melt them together. After one minute, stir the mixture and return to the microwave for one and a half minutes. If you are using an oven, bake them at 350⁰ F (180⁰ C) until they melt. If you are using a hot plate, stir constantly until the chips melt.

2. When the chocolate chips are melted, add the chow mein noodles.

3. Mix the noodles by using the spoons or forks as though you were tossing a salad. Be gentle, but be sure to coat each noodle with the chocolate chip and peanut butter mixture.

4. Put wax paper over the trays.

5. With a spoon, drop small clusters of the mixture on the covered trays.

6. Add a few valentine candies to the top of each cluster.

7. If you have a refrigerator, place the trays in it. The clusters will harden faster and be ready to eat sooner.

My Heart Book

by Ireta Sitts Graube

Summary

This is an easy to read book with a repetitive sentence structure. Through a series of statements about the heart, the book asks children to think about the heart, its structure, and its function. Children enjoy the simple format and love reading the book to their friends and families. My Heart Book *in big and little format is ready for you to duplicate on pages 30-40.*

The outline below is a suggested plan for using the various activities that are presented in this unit. You should adapt these ideas to fit your own classroom situations.

Sample Plan

Day 1

- Read Paul Showers' book *Hear Your Heart.* (see bibliography)
- Using the large copy of *My Heart Book,* begin reading the pages to the children and doing the activities listed in the Overview of Activities on page 29.
- Do Heart Location Art on page 41.
- Begin an exercise chart. (page 58)
- Freeze fruit cubes. (page 72)

Day 2

- Continue reading the book and doing activities in Overview.
- Do activities with seeing and feeling the pulse. (page 60)
- Play Keep Your Heart Healthy. (pages 44-46)
- Learn about the muscles with muscle movements. (page 61)
- Teach the song "Muscles Help You Move." (page 70)

Day 3

- Continue reading the book and doing the activities.
- Do Healthy Heart Sign Writing. (page 50)

- Make Frozen Banana Sticks. (page 72)
- Look at Veins & Arteries. (page 43)
- Begin a Pictograph. (page 48)
- Play Heart Rhythm Movement. (page 70)

Day 4

- Continue reading the book and doing the activities.
- Look at the heart as a pump. (page 42)
- Learn the song, "This is the Way the Heart Pumps Blood." (page 69)
- Do the heart pump experiment. (page 59)
- Begin some of the Healthy Heart writing activities on page 47.

Day 5

- Finish the book and the activities.
- Continue to do writing activities. (page 47)
- Make a Healthy & Non-Healthy Food Collage. (page 64)
- Sing all the songs you learned in this unit. (pages 67-70)

Overview of Activities

SETTING THE STAGE

1. Collect information and kits from the American Heart Association. Look in your yellow pages for the number in your area.

2. Get books on the heart from the library.

3. Make a copy of the class book on pages 30-37. You may enlarge these to 12" x 24" (30 cm x 61 cm) or glue the pages on large construction paper. If time permits, color the pictures or have a parent help you assemble the book.

4. Make copies for each student of the small book. Fold in the correct order.

5. Read *Hear Your Heart* by Paul Showers. See the bibliography, page 80.

6. Ask parents to save toilet paper rolls for the class to use to hear each other's hearts. (See below.)

ENJOYING THE BOOK

These activities and the reading of this book can be done over several days.

1. Read the first page of *My Heart Book*. Have the children find a partner. Provide one toilet paper roll for every two children. They can take turns hearing each other's heart.

2. Read the second page and let children practice feeling for their own pulses. The best place to feel a pulse is the wrist or under the chin on the neck. Use the water activity on page 59 to demonstrate the pulse. Read page 60 for more information on locating the pulse.

3. Read the third page. Close your fist and show the children the approximate size of the human heart. Have them place their closed fists over the left side of their chests to show the location of the heart.

4. Show the picture on page 43 and discuss the veins. Help the children to locate a vein on their body. Read the fourth page to the children and let them write in the answer. Color the veins blue.

5. Show the picture on page 43 to the children and discuss the arteries. Read the fifth page aloud and let the children fill in the answer. Color the arteries red.

6. Show the picture on page 42 to the class. What is the name of the little doors? Read page 6 of *My Heart Book* and let the children fill in the answer.

7. Discuss how fast hearts beat in human beings and animals (100-120 beats per minute in young children, 60-100 beats per minute in adults, 1,000 times per minute in a hamster). Using a watch with a second hand, time the children for one minute as they count their heartbeats. Read the last page of the book and write the number of heart beats on that page.

EXTENDING THE BOOK

1. Reread the little books to partners. Let the children color them.

2. Continue reading books about the heart. See page 80 for suggestions.

3. Do the experiments on pages 59-61 that involve the heart action.

4. Play the Heart Healthy game on pages 44-46.

5. Start the healthy eating chart for the class. See page 48.

My Heart Book

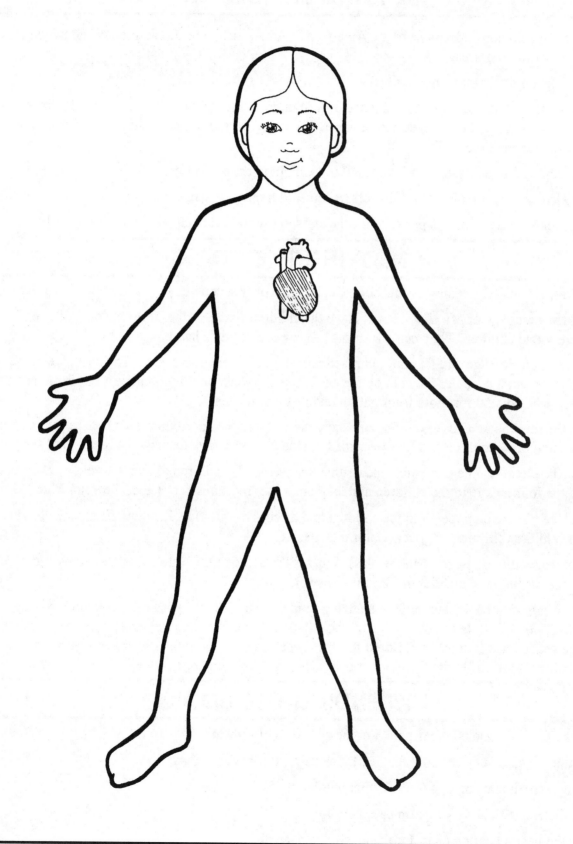

What do I know about my heart?

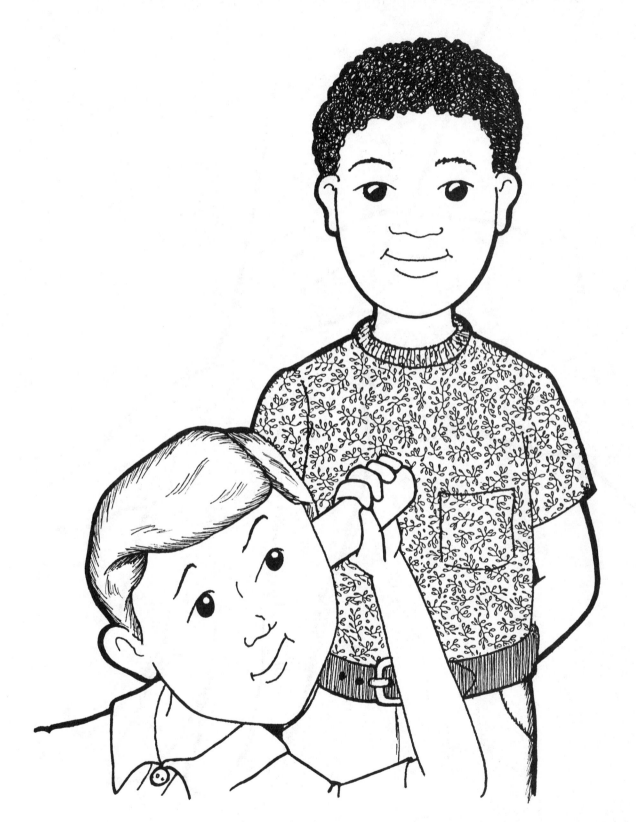

I know I can hear my heart beat.

2

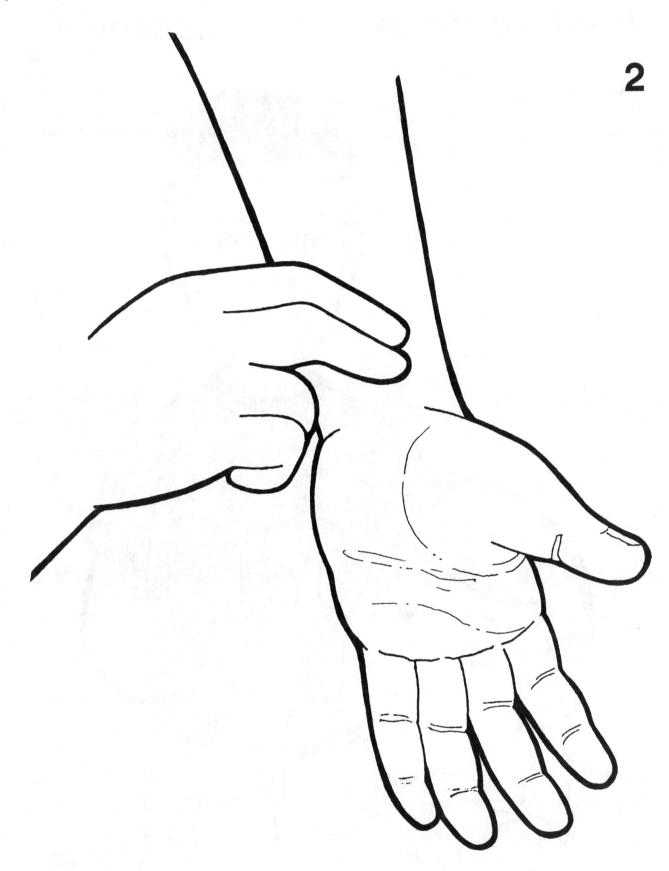

I know I can feel my heart beat.

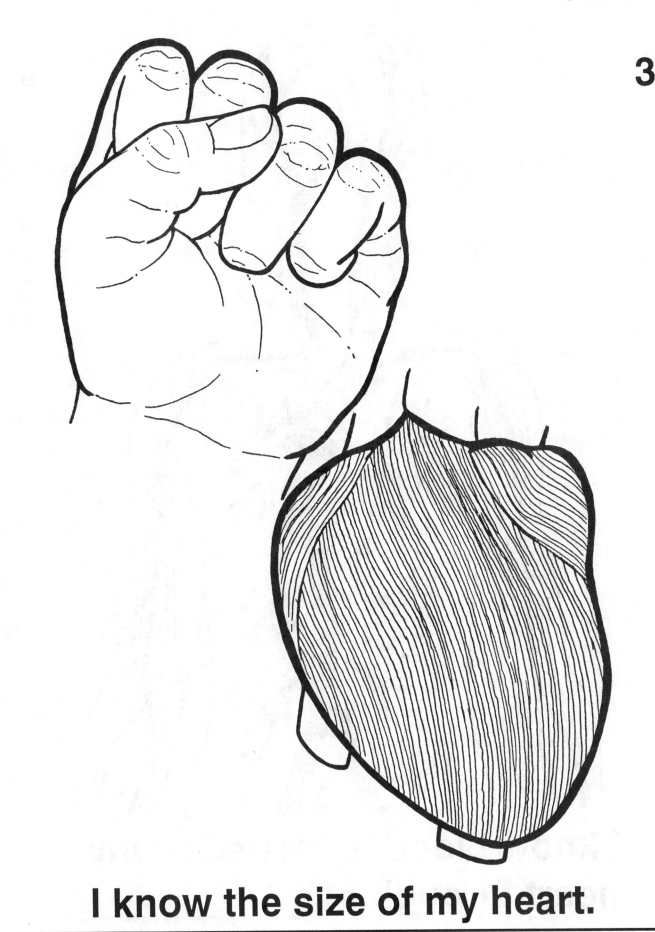

I know the size of my heart.

4

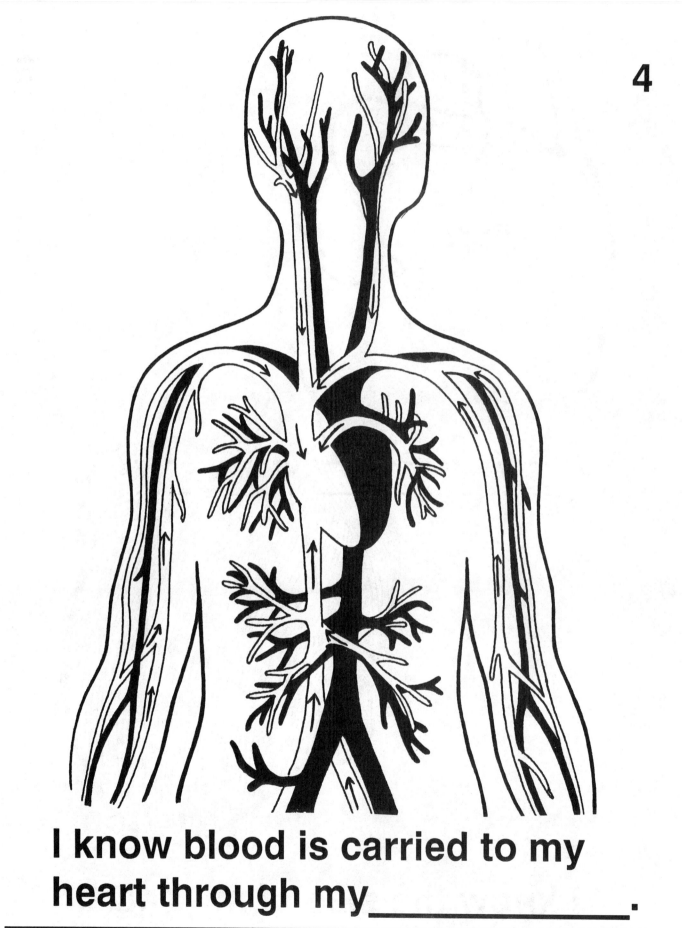

I know blood is carried to my heart through my _____.

34

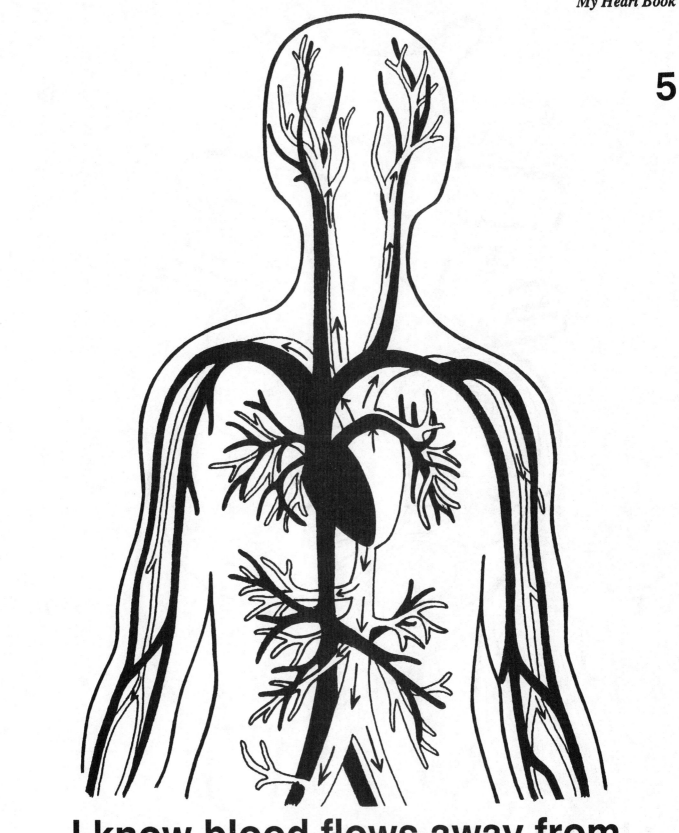

I know blood flows away from my heart through my _____.

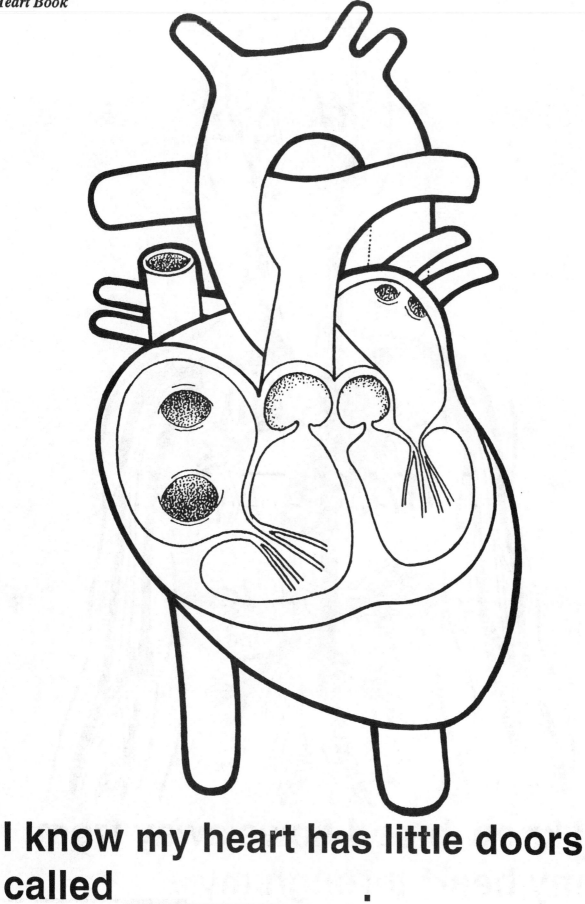

I know my heart has little doors called _____.

I know my heart beats about _____ times every minute. I know a lot about my heart.

How To Make the Little Book

What do you know about your heart? Ask children this question. Then use the little book on pages 39 and 40 after you have studied and read about the heart. This book will help children review what they have learned.

Materials: copies of the little book for each child (pages 39 and 40); crayons or colored pencils

Directions: Pass out the pages to each child and let them fold and staple it to make a little book. If they need help reading it, read it together. Discuss pages 5, 6, 7, and 8. Let them fill in the answers by using crayons or colored pencils. Color in the pictures.

Extension: Make a Big Book just like the little book. The pictures may be enlarged and glued to large paper. Let students take the Big Book home to share with families.

❶

❷

❸

❹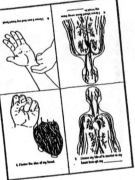

❺

❻

❼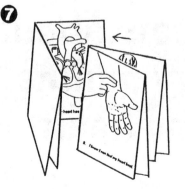

❽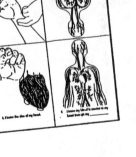

Little Book

I know my heart has little doors
called _____.

7

I know I can hear my heart beat.

2

8

I know my heart beats about
_____ times every minute.
I know a lot about my heart.

1

What do I know about my heart?

Little Book (cont.)

I know I can feel my heart beat.

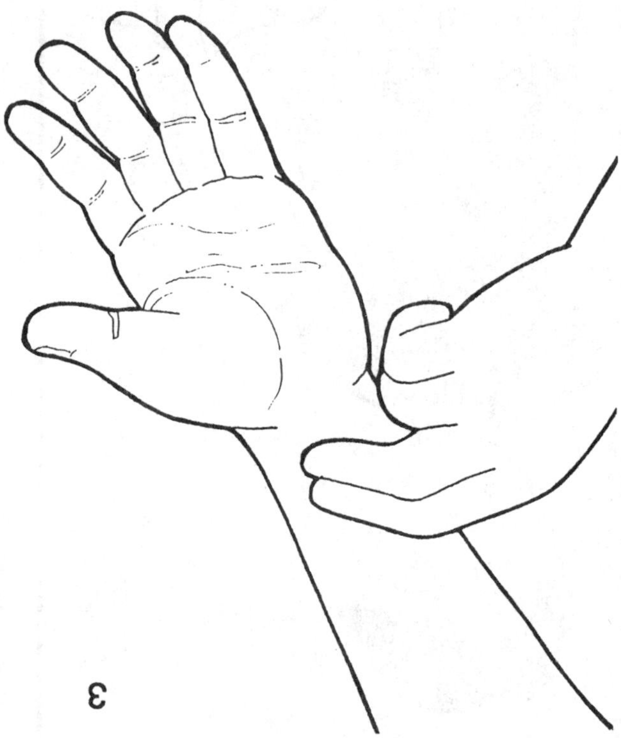

3

I know blood flows away from my heart in _____.

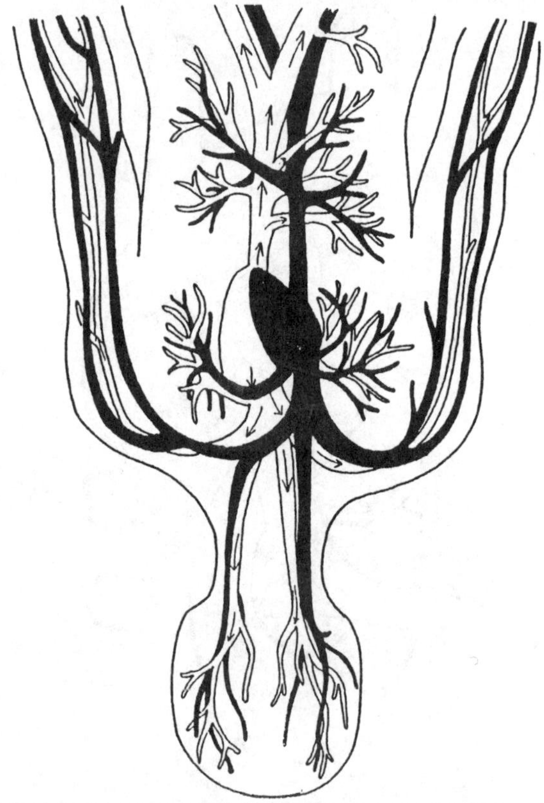

9

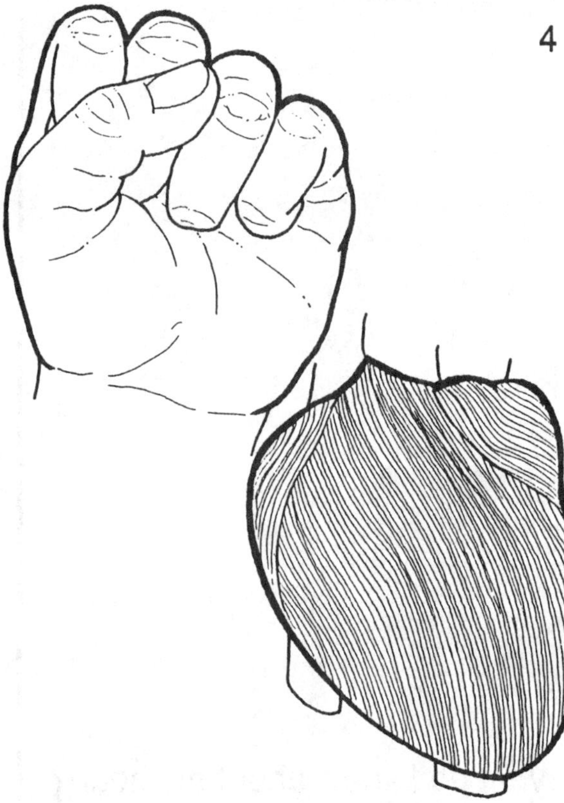

I know the size of my heart.

4

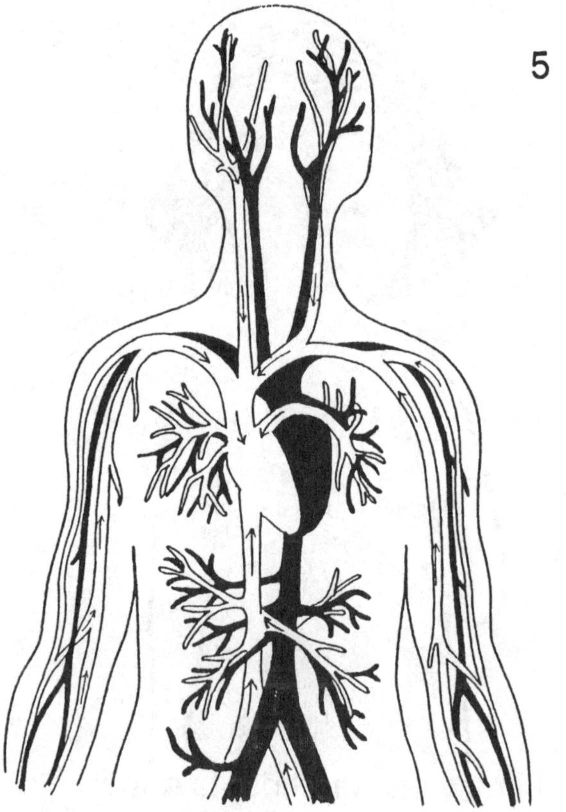

I know my blood is carried to my heart through my _____.

5

Heart Location and Size

Materials: large piece of butcher paper for each child; crayons or oil crayons; pencils; scissors

Directions: Ask the children to close their right fists and place them over the left side of their chests. Move the fists a little toward the center. This is the location of their hearts and their fists are the approximate size of their hearts.

Let the children choose a partner or assign partners. Have one child lie down on the butcher paper while the other traces around the outline of the child. Trade places and let the other child trace around the partner on another sheet of butcher paper. After both partners are traced on paper, have them determine where the heart is located on each child and, using a pencil, draw it in place. Older children may want to draw veins and arteries going to and from the heart and color all the arteries red and the veins blue.

Variations: Add muscles, lungs, etc. to the bodies.

The Heart as a Pump

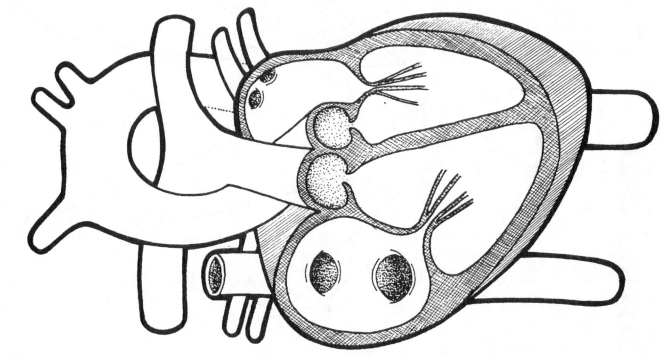

Teacher Information: The heart is really two pumps. The right side of the heart sends blood to the lungs. The left side of the heart sends blood to the other body organs. The two sides are separated by a muscle wall. Each side of the heart has two small rooms or chambers. The upper room is like a little bag. The lower room is much larger and has stronger walls. The rooms are connected by a little door called a valve. This little door opens and closes, letting blood in and out of the room.

Give each child a copy of the heart on the right. It might be helpful to draw a picture of the heart (see box) on the chalkboard or an overhead projector as you explain the parts of the heart to the children. Ask the children to label the parts of the heart.

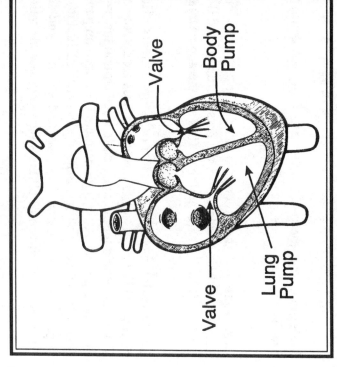

Valve

Valve

Body Pump

Lung Pump

42

Veins and Arteries

Teacher Information: *(Read this to the children.)*

If we took all of your blood vessels out of your body and joined them together, they would extend for nearly 94,000 miles. That is halfway to the moon.

The vessels that carry blood away from your heart are called the arteries. The vessels that carry blood back to your heart are called veins. You can see veins through your skin on the underside of your wrist.

We call your heart and all your blood vessels your circulatory system.

Materials: copy of this page, blue and red crayons

Directions: Color all the dark vessels blue. These are your veins. They carry blood back to your heart. Color all the light vessels red. These are your arteries. They carry blood away from your heart to all parts of your body.

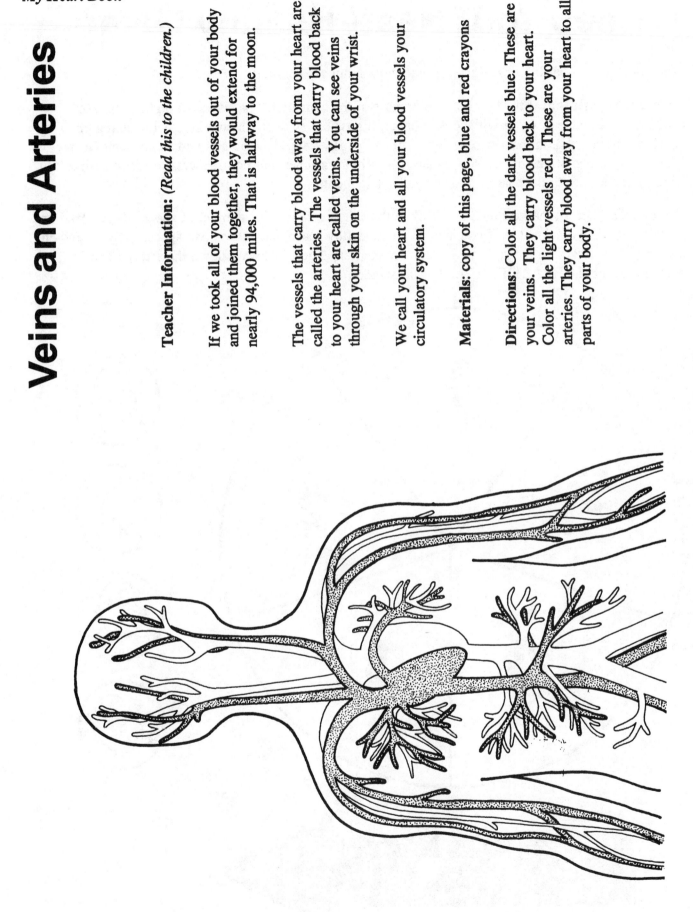

Keep Your Heart Healthy Game

Materials: game board; four markers; spinner with numbers 1-5 on it.

Teacher Preparation: If time permits, color parts of the game. Glue pages 45-46 on tag board or cardboard. Laminate or cover with contact paper, if possible. Cut out the markers below and glue to tag board or cardboard. Laminate or cover with contact paper. Reproduce pointer and spinner onto heavy paper. Cut out and attach pointer to spinner using a brad fastener. For non-readers, you may wish to add a happy or sad face to the healthy and unhealthy statements.

Directions: Place all markers on START. Spin the spinner. Move that number of spaces. If you land on a healthy space, you can stay. If you land on an unhealthy space, move back two spaces. If you land on a vein, slide forward on the vein. If you land on an artery, slide backward down the artery. The first person to reach the HEALTHY HEART is the winner.

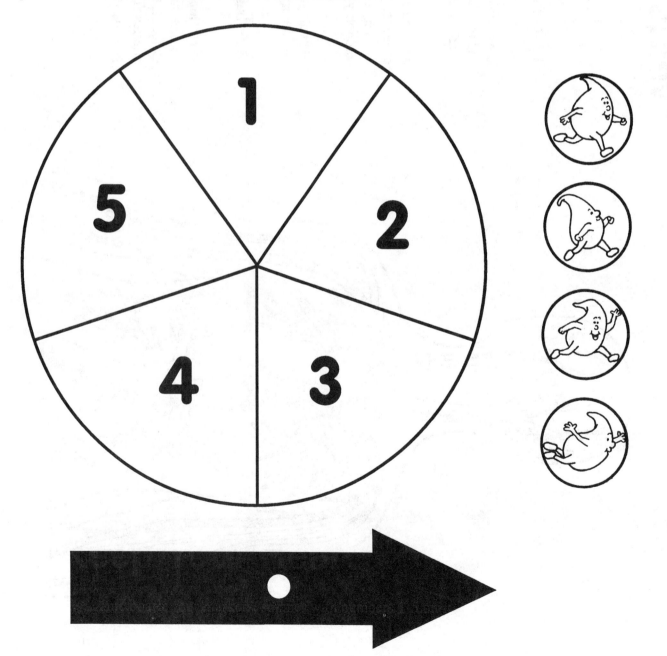

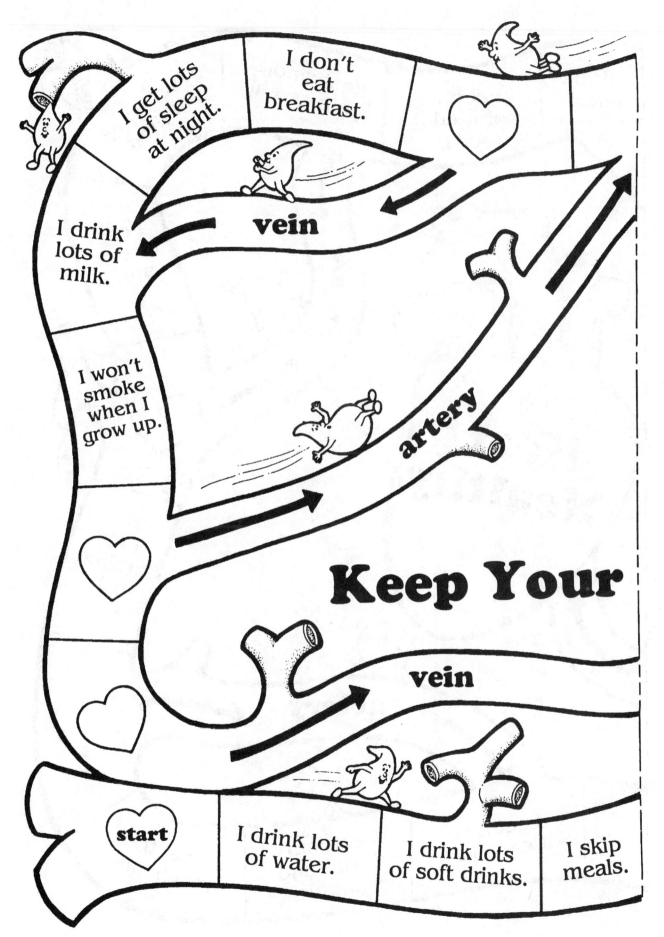

Keep Your

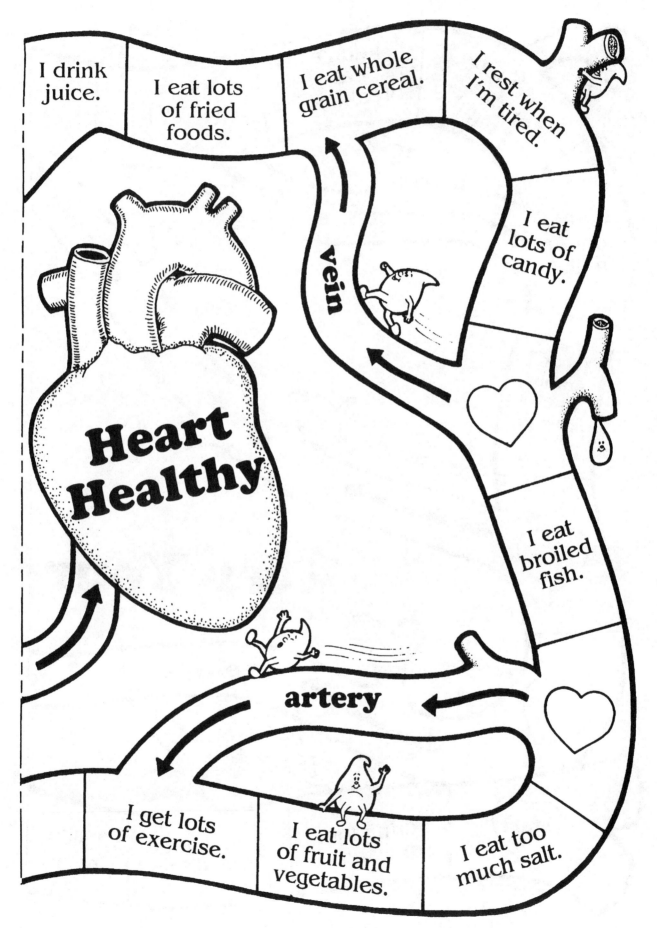

Healthy Heart

Try writing some of these healthy heart ideas.

Shopping List

~~soda pop~~
cereal
~~butter~~
milk
strawberries
~~candy~~

1. Make a grocery shopping list with heart healthy foods and some that are not healthy. Trade papers with someone. Have that person correct your list, by finding and crossing out the items that are not heart healthy.

2. Write a menu for one day's breakfast, lunch, and dinner with heart healthy foods. Trade with another student and check the menu. How would you improve it? Did they include fruits and vegetables and plenty of milk?

3. Look at your menu. Choose two items and write a recipe for each one. Be sure to include directions as well as ingredients.

4. List the ways you can keep your heart healthy. How many ways can you think of? How does each item keep your heart healthy?

5. Write a T.V. advertisement telling people how to keep their hearts healthy. Read it to the class with expression. Make sure you are selling your ideas to the class. Do they believe you?

6. Make a diagram of the heart and show how blood flows in and out. Label the parts.

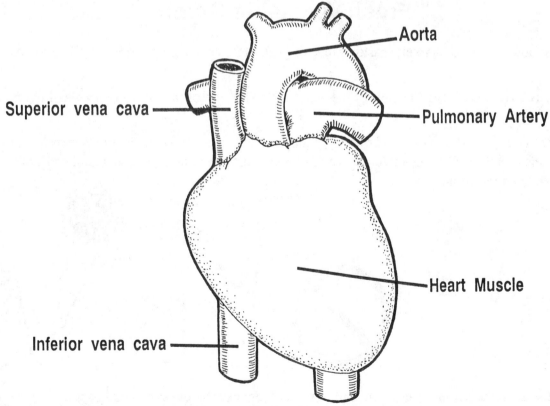

Aorta

Superior vena cava

Pulmonary Artery

Heart Muscle

Inferior vena cava

7. Make a tape recorded message telling people how important exercise is for a healthy heart. Tell what exercise you get now and what exercise you plan to do when you are an adult.

Healthy Eating for Your Heart

Breakfast Chart

Give each child a copy of the graph on Monday to keep in the classroom. Let each student fill it out daily upon arriving in class. Fill in with yes or no on each day. The purpose of the chart is to help students realize that eating a healthy breakfast helps them function better and helps keep their hearts healthy. After keeping the chart for one month, children can analyze which days of the week they need to change eating habits.

I ate a healthy breakfast.							
Week of							
	Sun.	Mon.	Tues.	Wed.	Thurs.	Fri.	Sat.

Fresh Vegetable Graph

Materials: butcher paper; marker; masking tape or push pins; vegetable patterns below; crayons; scissors

Teacher Preparation: Write the days of the week on the bottom of the butcher paper and the number of students up the side.

Directions: Take a class survey. Find out how many students ate a fresh vegetable yesterday. Give each child that answered "yes" a vegetable pattern. Let them color and cut out the vegetable. Glue it on the chart above the appropriate day.

Variations: Turn the survey over to the children. Let them ask the questions and pass out the patterns. Use a different question daily or weekly. Did you eat fresh fruit, whole grains, such as bread or cereal, non-fried foods, low-fat milk, etc.? Use the patterns above to create a pictograph.

48

Writing Skits and Dramatizations

Materials: paper, pencils, props, books on the heart, healthy eating, and muscles

Directions: Divide the class into groups of 4. Give each group one of the following assignments. They must write and then act out a skit or a dramatization of the problem. This may be a pantomime or a skit with words.

• How do the different body muscles work? One person could be a skeletal muscle that moves part of the arm. Another person could be a skeletal muscle that moves a part of the face. Another person might be a smooth muscle that moves food down the throat and the last person could be the heart muscle. Show what your job is and guess which muscle you are pretending to be.

• What path does blood take around your body? Write your script down first. One person is the heart, one the veins, one the arteries, and one the blood. Show how the blood moves and what paths it takes to get around the body.

• This person has eaten too much fat. What is happening in the arteries? Write how you will act this out. One person is the artery, one the blood, one the heart, and one is the vein.

• This person doesn't exercise and eats the wrong kinds of food. Write a play telling us the effects of these actions on this person's heart. Pretend to be the blood, heart, muscles, and arteries of this person.

• This person is a smoker. Write the script and then pretend to be the heart, lungs, blood, and arteries.

• How does the heart work? Write about the structure of the heart. Pretend to be the upper and lower chambers and the valves that open and close. Show us how you work to pump blood.

• What happens to the heart when a heart attack occurs? Write the script and then pretend to be the doctor, patient, and family members.

Invite the principal, secretary, parents, or another class to see these dramatizations. Or present these skits at Open House.

Healthy Heart

Sign Writing

Materials: writing paper; tag board, railroad board, or any heavy paper or cardboard; crayons; marking pens; paints; glue; scraps of colored paper; masking tape; push pins

Directions: What do we need to do to keep our hearts healthy? As the children list some of the things they've learned, write the list on the board or on an overhead projector. Let the children choose paper and make signs to post around the classroom or the school. These signs will help remind the students how to take care of their hearts.

Extensions: Let the children choose one or two rules they think their own families might need help with. Have them make signs to post in their own homes to help remind family members of their responsibility toward maintaining a healthy heart.

Valentine Poetry Writing

Materials: paper; pencil; book of valentine poems, *Good Morning to You, Valentine*. See bibliography for more information.

Directions: Read the poetry to the class. Have them listen for rhyming words and write them down when they hear them. Or write the words on the chalkboard or chart paper as the children hear them. Allow the children time to brainstorm additional rhyming words that might be used in writing valentine poems. Record these words.

When they are ready, let them write their own poems, using these rhyming words. Provide a time for each child to read one or two poems to the class or to a partner. Sharing one's work is an important part of writing and should always be a part of a writing experience.

More Writing Ideas

1. Write a valentine to a favorite book character.

2. Write a description of a good friend. This friend could be a person, pet, or an object. Tell the personality traits of the friend.

3. Draw a portrait of a friend. Complete this sentence as a caption for the portrait. "My friend is so much fun because _____."

Valentine Crossword Puzzle

Fill in the blank hearts with the right word.

Down

2. Something you give someone on Valentine's Day.

Across

1. What do you feel on Valentine's Day?
3. What do you eat on Valentine's Day?
4. A strong muscle in your chest.

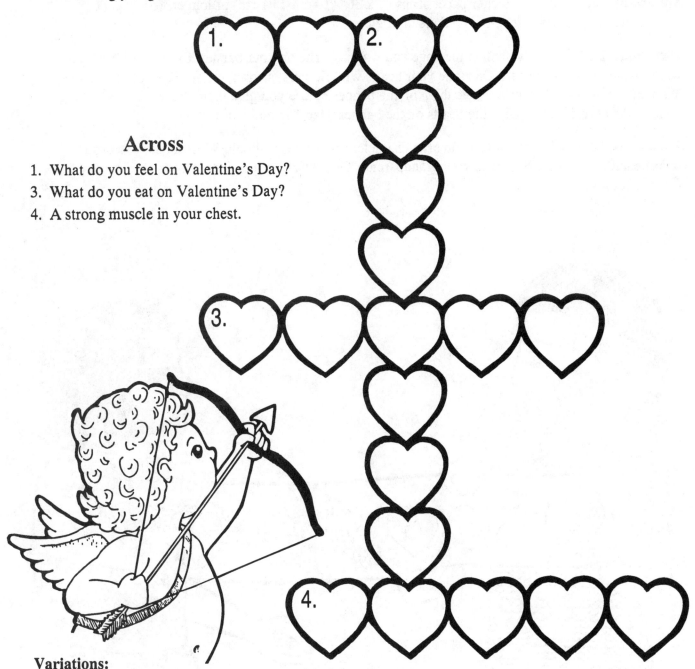

Variations:

1. What other words can you fit into this crossword puzzle? Write down the clues and pass it to a friend to solve.

2. Can you fit your first and\or last name in the puzzle anywhere? Your teacher's name? Your mom or dad?

3. Can you make a crossword puzzle using your family members' names or your classmates' names?

Valentine Banners

Teacher Preparation: Cut crepe paper or butcher paper in strips of approximately 4" x 36" (10 cm x 91 cm). This paper can be white or any color the children want for the background of their valentine banners.

Materials: crepe paper or butcher paper strips 4" x 36" (10 cm x 91 cm) or longer; red or pink construction paper; scissors; glue; markers or crayons

Directions: Decide what valentine message you want to write on your banner. Cut enough hearts to write one letter on each heart. Decorate your hearts with flowers, arrows, etc. Write a letter on each heart with crayons or markers. Place them on the banner before you glue them down. Be sure you get them in the correct order. Glue the hearts on the banner. Hang up and enjoy.

Variations: Write a banner to your favorite character in a valentine book. Write a banner to your favorite author. Write a banner to your grandparents. Or try writing a banner in code and let the class figure out the code.

52

Secret Valentine Math

Answer the equations below and figure out the secret message. Use the code at the bottom of the page to fill in the blank spaces with letters.

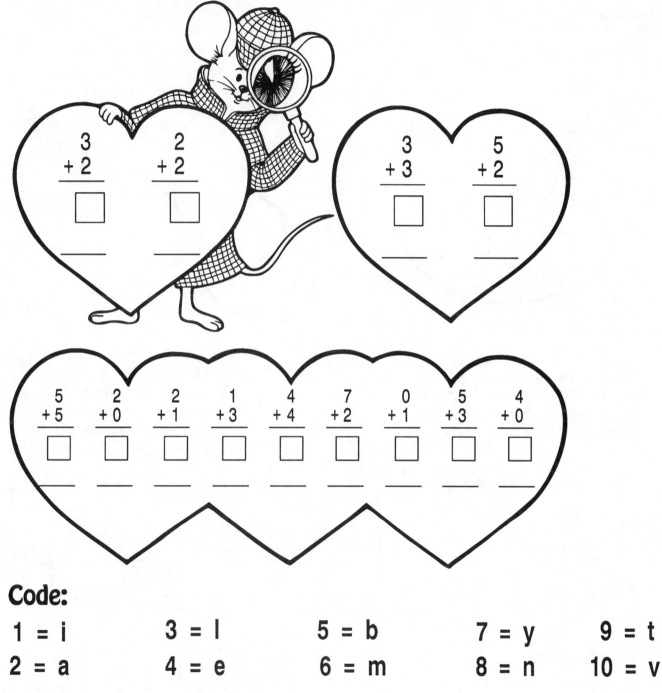

Code:

1 = i	3 = l	5 = b	7 = y	9 = t
2 = a	4 = e	6 = m	8 = n	10 = v

Variations:

1. Can you make up another secret message using other addition or subtraction facts? Send it to a classmate to decode.

2. Make up a secret code for your brother, sister, or parents. Take it home and let them figure it out!

Potato Print Math

Materials: raw potatoes; small sharp knife; tempera paint; flat container to hold paint; white or pink 9" x 12" (23 cm x 30 cm) construction paper; markers; pens or pencils

Directions:

1. Cut the potato in half.

2. Draw a pattern of a heart or an arrow on the surface of the cut side of the potato. Keep the design simple.

3. With a knife, cut away all the potato that is not part of the pattern. When you are finished, the pattern will be raised above the rest of the potato.

4. Dip the potato in the paint and print on your math paper. You will need to make addition or subtraction problems with the print and then write the equation on the bottom.

Variation:

1. Have the child first write the equation and then illustrate it with the potato print.

2. Use the potato prints to make valentine cards or pictures.

3. Make a valentine math book. Put a different equation on each page and illustrate the equations with the potato prints.

Hearts in Order

Color the hearts red. Cut and paste in order.

Count the Hearts

How many hearts can you see?
How many circles can you see?

There are _____ hearts.

There are _____ circles.

56

Pie Graph

Materials: chalk; paper; crayons; flat paved area on the playground

Directions: Ask how many children are wearing the valentine color, red. Those children will need to form a line and hold hands. The children not wearing red will form a line and hold hands. The children on the ends of each line will hold hands with the children of the other group and form a large circle. One child or the teacher will draw a circle around the inside of the children with chalk. Each group will be standing together on the edge of the chalk circle.

Have the children help locate the center of the circle and place an "X" in the center. Draw lines from the "X" to the beginning and ending of the red group. Which group makes the biggest piece of the pie? This is a pie chart.

Pass out crayons and papers and let each child copy one of the human pie graphs that you made on the playground. This can be done right on the playground so the child can remember what a pie graph looks like. Label the pie chart.

Variation: Divide the class by hair color, eye color, velcro versus tie shoes, number of siblings, or birth order. Show the children more complicated pie graphs using more than one category.

Graphing and Map Reading

Exercise and Your Heart

Teacher Information: Hearts can be strengthened by regular physical activities. The heart will pump more blood per beat when it is fit. This allows the heart to beat at a slower rate. Physical activity also improves blood circulation throughout the body. The heart, lungs, and other organs work together more effectively. Physical activity also helps control weight and reduce stress.

Materials: local maps and or mileage charts; 9" x 12" (23 cm x 30 cm) paper; crayons; pencils

Directions: Pretend you are going to ride your bicycle from your school to nearby cities to get exercise. Keep a mileage chart of how far you are riding. Graph how many miles you would need to go to get to each city.

Variations: Use blocks instead of miles within a city.

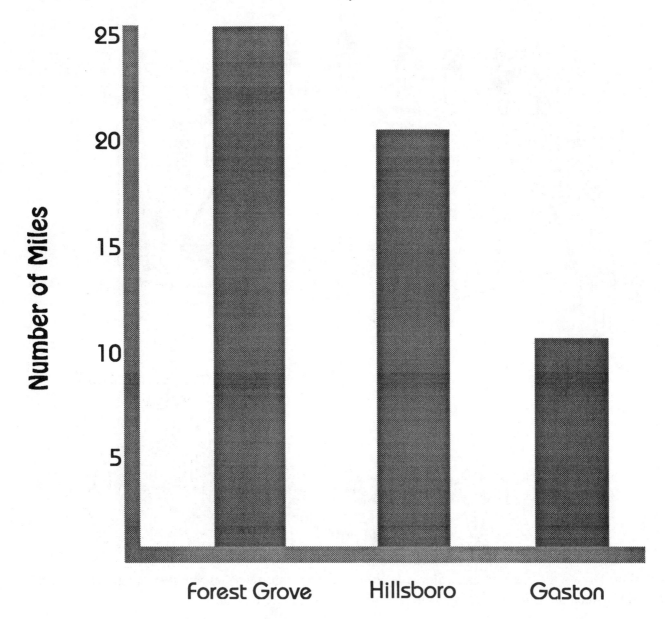

How a Heart Pumps

Teacher Information: To demonstrate the action of the heart muscle, let the children squeeze water through their hands, relax, and squeeze again. Each beat of the heart pumps about a cup full of blood.

Materials: plastic bucket, pan, or sink; water

Directions: Fill the bucket half full of water. Let the children cup their hands together under water. Have them squeeze their hands together. Water will squirt out. Relax the hands and let the water fill them again. Repeat this action to understand how the heart works.

Variation: Cut a small hole in a racquetball or tennis ball and fill it with water. Squeeze the ball and the water will squirt out. Relax your hand and the ball will return to its original shape. Fill it again and repeat. This is the same as your heart action. The heart squeezes blood out to the parts of the body. When it relaxes, it fills with blood again and gets ready to squeeze again.

1. Cut hole.

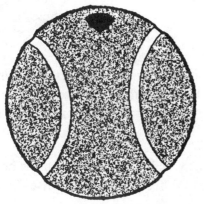

2. Fill ball with water.

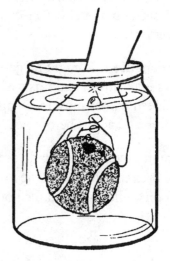

3. Squeeze ball and water squirts out.

4. Relax grip on ball and fill with water again.

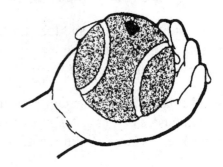

How a Heart Pumps *(cont.)*

Seeing and Feeling the Pulse

To visually demonstrate the movement of the blood through the body, let the children try this experiment.

Teacher Information: Explain the term "pulse." As the heart pumps blood through the body, you can feel the surging of the blood. This up and down motion that you feel is called your pulse.

Materials: tape; paper clip

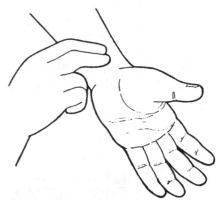

Directions: Have the children put their left arms on the desks, palm side up. Find their pulses by feeling with the second and third finger of the right hand just below the base of the thumb or on their wrists. If they can't find it at first, move the fingers around. When they find the pulse, place a loop of tape with a paper clip on it on top of the pulse. Watch the clip move! It's fascinating for children to see this movement.

Teacher Information: It might be good for the teacher to demonstrate this activity first on his/herself. Adult pulses move slower and it is easier for the children to see this movement. For some reason, this experiment doesn't work on some people. You simply can't see the pulse using this method. Try several children and adults before you give up!

It is really impressive, when you do see the pulse move. Feel the pulse in various parts of the body. Have the children use the second and third finger of the right hand in feeling for their pulse. Let them practice first on themselves and then on a partner.

Directions:

1. Feel on either side of your neck just below the jaw.

2. Feel the pulse on the inside of your ankle next to your ankle bone.

3. Feel the pulse under your arm in your armpit.

4. Feel the pulse on your temple, right at the hair line.

Find their resting pulse first and then try jumping up and down twenty times and retaking their pulse. What happens to the pulse when they exercise?

Additional information: An adult's heart beats 60-100 and a child's heart beats 100-120 times a minute. A mouse's or a hamster's heart beats about 1000 times a minute. A dog's heart beats about 150 times and a horse's beats 30 times a minute. Large animals usually have slower heartbeats than smaller animals.

The Heart As a Muscle

To help children understand how muscles work in the body, let them do the following exercises. You may wish to have mirrors available.

Ask the children to run in place, smile, touch their toes, etc. When you ran, you used muscles in your legs. When you smiled, you used muscles in your face, and when you touched your toes, you used muscles in your arms. Every time you move any part of your body, you use a muscle. We have over 600 muscles in our body. Some are very big and some are very small.

There are several types of muscles in our body. Some muscles are skeletal muscles. They are fastened to the bones of your skeleton. When you moved your body and smiled, you were using skeletal muscles. Smooth muscles are in your throat, stomach, and your eye. What would smooth muscles do in your throat? *(Help swallow food.)* What would smooth muscles do in your stomach? *(Help digest food.)* What would smooth muscles do in your eye? *(Change the size of your pupil to let in more light or take in less light.)*

Stand up and bend over and put your hands around your right leg just above the knee. Hold onto your leg as you walk. Can you feel the muscle moving? It is pulling up and down as you walk. This is a skeletal muscle at work. Flex your arms like a body builder. Can you feel and see your arm muscle move?

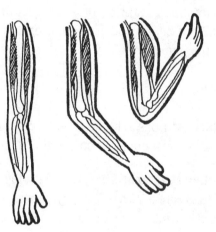

Watch in a mirror as you make faces. Your face has 16 different muscles that work together to produce all the hundreds of different expressions you can make.

Drink a glass of water or eat a cracker. Your smooth throat muscles are working to swallow the water and food, and your stomach muscles are working to digest the food. Turn off the lights in the room. Your smooth eye muscles are working to take in more light.

Your heart muscle is not any of these types of muscles. It is a special muscle that works every minute of your life. The heart is a pump muscle and pumps hundreds and hundreds of gallons of blood every day. If your heart and your smooth muscles are healthy, they never get tired. Skeletal muscles get tired and need to rest for a bit, but all muscles need to work to stay strong and healthy.

Valentine Checkers and Checkerboard

Checkers

Materials: play dough (recipe follows); heart pattern template (see below); cardboard or tag board; wax paper; butter or plastic knife; pink and red tempera paint; rolling pin; lacquer or clear nail polish; candy conversation hearts (optional); pink and red construction paper (optional)

Directions: Make a class set of valentine checkers to keep in the classroom by having each student make 3-4 checkers. Give each child a ball of play dough. Have him or her roll it out on the wax paper. Using the template and the knife, children should cut out the hearts. They will need to harden and dry for 3-4 days or they may be baked in an oven at 350° F (180° C) for 1 hour or until hard. When the hearts are dry, have the children paint them, painting 12 pink and 12 red. To make them shiny, paint with lacquer or clear finger nail polish. Keep these checkers in the classroom for use at school.

Children may make a take-home set of checkers by using red and pink construction paper and cutting out 12 red hearts and 12 pink hearts. Or you may give them 24 candy hearts of two different colors to play the game.

Checkerboard

Materials: For each child: 1 piece of red construction paper (mat), 12" x 14" (30 cm x 40 cm); twelve 1" x 12" (2.54 cm x 30 cm) white strips of construction paper; scissors; tape, glue, or paste

Teacher Preparation: Before giving the red mats to the children, prepare the mats by folding them in half to create a 7" x 12" mat. Starting at the fold, make eleven cuts, each 1" in width. Cut to one inch from the top edge of the paper. When the paper is unfolded, students will have a mat ready for weaving.

Directions: Give students a prepared mat, and twelve 1" x 12" strips of white construction paper. Show them how to weave in and out, alternating starting under and over weaving with each new strip. This will create a pattern of alternating red and white strips. When all the white strips are woven, glue the ends down. When this is finished, children should fold the red border under and glue or tape it.

Play Dough Recipe

4 cups (472 mL) flour

1 cup (236 mL) salt

1 ½ cups (354 mL) water

Mix the dough until it is stiff. Knead it for five minutes. Keep it in an air tight container until you are ready to use it. Double this recipe for the heart checkers. There will be some dough left over for children to make their own hearts to take home or play with in the classroom.

Valentine Love Bug

Make a love bug with a hidden message for your Valentine.

1. Reproduce, color and cut out. Write a secret message on the body.

2. To attach the head and wings, poke a brad through the head at A; through left wing at A; through the body at A. Attach the other side by poking a brad through the head at B; through the right wing at B; through the body at B.

3. Now you can give it to your Valentine.

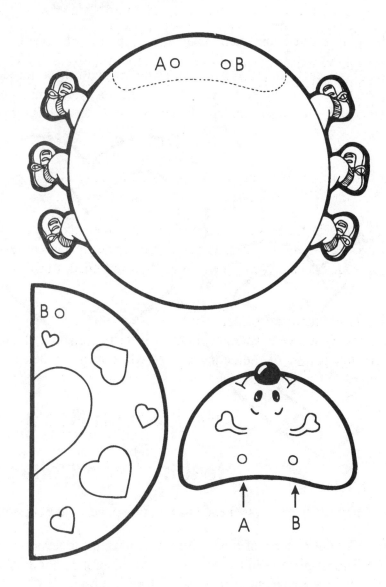

Unique Valentines

This Is Your Life

Materials: magazines; 18" x 24" (46 cm x 61 cm) construction paper; glue; scissors; scrap box filled with any decoration notions

Directions: Think about the people you want to give these valentines to. What do they like to do? What foods do they like to eat? What music do they like? Do you have any photographs of them? Look through the magazines. Cut out anything that reminds you of the people you are making the gift for. Arrange everything on the construction paper. Make it look as nice as possible. Glue it down. Add bits of ribbon, paper hearts, doilies, etc. Write a special poem or note and glue it on the paper. This will be a very special gift.

Heart Links

Materials: pink and red construction paper; heart patterns below

Directions: Give each student 1 sheet of pink hearts and 1 sheet of red hearts. Have them cut out the hearts. Then have them cut out the center of the hearts by cutting up on the bottom one. Link the hearts together (red-pink-red-pink) then tape the bottom of the heart back together. Use them to decorate the classroom.

Healthy Heart Collage

Materials: magazines or newspapers; construction paper; glue; scissors

Directions: Cut out pictures of food from the magazines or newspapers that you think would be heart healthy. Hide some pictures in the collage that would not be good for your heart. Trade papers with a friend. Can they find the pictures that are not heart healthy?

Variations: Write the names on the food and a Yes if they are healthy and a No if they are not.

Pin Prick Pictures

Materials: push pins (one per child); copies of patterns on pages 65 and 66 (enough so each child can do 2-3 pictures); carpet, carpet squares or magazines; paper clips; 9" x 12"(23 cm x 30 cm) red and pink construction paper; stapler (optional) and staple remover

Directions: Securely paper clip one of the patterns on pages 65 and 66 on top of a piece of construction paper. Punch holes with the push pin all the way around the outline of the picture. The holes should be about $1/16$-$1/8$ inches apart. Use the carpet or a magazine on the other side of the paper to cushion the pin pricks. When finished, remove the pattern and hold the picture up to a window. The picture will shine through the holes.

Note: If the pattern is allowed to shift, the picture will be distorted. If paper clips do not hold it securely enough, staple the pattern to the construction paper. Remove the staple with a staple remover when the picture is finished.

Pin Prick Pictures *(cont.)*

Musical Activities

Feel the Music

Materials: a recording or tape of happy, instrumental music with no words (about 3-5 minutes long); construction paper; crayons

Optional: warming tray; peeled crayons; plain white paper

Directions: Play the recording and let the children listen to the music. Let them express the movement of the music by moving their hands.

Play the recording again and this time let them move a crayon on paper with the same motions. When the music stops, they must stop and the picture is complete.

Variations: Purchase or borrow a warming tray. (They can be purchased at second hand shops.) Plug in the warming tray and place a sheet of paper on it. Let the children move peeled crayons over the paper. The crayon melts as they move it on the warmed surface. It has a wonderful flowing feeling as your hand glides over the surface while the crayon melts. The music in the background helps to create a work of art!

Chanting

Chanting is an important part of the musical development of a child. A feeling for rhyme is increased. Children love the familiarity of repetition in words and songs. It gives them confidence to be able to repeat a chant.

Materials: The following chant, or any other which you or the children have made up. The chant can be printed on the chalkboard or chart paper or just read to the children.

Directions: Chant the verse three times. The first in a speaking voice, the second in a very loud voice, and the last in a very soft voice.

Roses are red,

Violets are blue.

Valentine, valentine,

I love you!

    or

Valentine, Valentine, I like you.

Valentine, Valentine, it's so true!

Variations:

1. Have part of the class chant one part of the poem and another part chant the last part.

2. Chant in echo fashion. The teacher says it first and the students echo.

3. Draw a light or dark line on the chalkboard to indicate when the students should use loud or soft voices.

Musical Activities *(cont.)*

Listening Music

Materials: tape or record of softly flowing music; red and white crepe paper streamers or scarves (optional)

Directions: Let the children find a space by themselves in the classroom. They can move their bodies to the music, but not their feet. Let them wave crepe paper streamers or scarves for a beautiful effect.

Freeze Valentine

Materials: one valentine for each child, simple recording or tape with a steady beat

Directions: Each child finds a place in the room where he or she can move. As the music is played, the children walk to the steady beat. When the music stops (you stop the tape or record) the children drop their valentines and freeze. When the music continues the children walk with the beat and pick up another child's valentine, not their own, and continue until the next freeze.

Songs From and For the Heart

Do You Know My Valentine?

Tune: "The Muffin Man"

Do you know my valentine,
My valentine, my valentine?
Do you know my valentine
Who has the pretty brown eyes?

Continue the song describing a child in the classroom, e.g.:

Who has a pretty blue dress?
Who has the shiny brown hair?

Continue this until the children can guess which child you are describing.

Variation: This can also be a circle game, with one child standing in the center. When that child thinks he knows who the person being described is, he or she will skip over and take that child's hand and skip around the circle with him or her. The new child will then get to be the next one to guess who is being described in the song.

68

Musical Activities *(cont.)*

This is the Way the Heart Pumps Blood

Tune: "Here We Go Round the Mulberry Bush"

Use this song to teach about the heart.

This is the way the heart pumps blood, heart pumps blood, heart pumps blood.

This is the way the heart pumps blood, ev'ry day.

This is how the blood comes in, blood comes in, blood comes in. This is how the blood comes in, ev'ry day.

This is how the blood goes out, blood goes out, blood goes out.

This is how the blood goes out, ev'ry day.

Use this verse to teach about the arteries.

Arteries carry blood away from your heart, away from your heart, away from your heart.

Arteries carry blood away from your heart, ev'ry day.

Veins carry blood back to your heart, back to your heart, back to your heart.

Veins carry blood back to your heart, ev'ry day.

As a group activity, divide children into groups of four. Three children make a circle by holding hands and forming the heart. The fourth child is the blood and comes in and goes out with the song. The children forming the heart squeeze together when they are forcing blood (child) out, and open the circle when they are letting blood (child) in.

As an individual activity, have each child place two hands together with finger tips touching to show opening and closing of the heart muscle.

You Are Mine

Tune: "A Tisket, A Tasket"

You are mine, you are mine,

A red and white valentine.

I wrote a letter to my love

And on the way I dropped it

I dropped it

I dropped it

And on the way I dropped it.

_____ *picked it up*

(Child's first and last name)

And put it in his/her pocket.

Directions: The children stand in a circle holding hands. One child is outside the circle with a valentine. As the children sing the song this child skips around the circle and drops the valentine in back of another child. This child then continues to skip around the circle and takes the place of the child who dropped the valentine in back of him or her in the circle. The other child picks up the valentine and continues the game.

Musical Activities *(cont.)*

Muscles Help You Move

Tune: Sally's Wearing a Red Dress

Muscles help you move, move, move,
Move, move, move,
Move, move, move.
Muscles help you move, move, move
All day long.
Skeletal muscles move your bones,
Move your bones,
Move your bones.
Skeletal muscles move your bones
All day long.
Smooth muscles move your throat,
Eyes and stomach,
Eyes and stomach,
Smooth muscles move in your body
All day long.
The heart muscle will move your blood,
Move your blood,
Move your blood.
The heart muscle will move your blood
All life long.

Directions: Point to various parts of the body as the children sing. Or have a picture of the body on a bulletin board and let children take turns pointing to various body parts as they sing the song.

I Am Making Valentines

Tune: London Bridge

I am making valentines,
Valentines, valentines.
I am making valentines.
Aren't they pretty?
I am using red paper,
Red paper, red paper.
I am using red paper.
Aren't they pretty?
I will send one right to you,
Right to you, right to you.
I will send one right to you.
My dear valentine!

Rhythms of the Heart

The beating of the heart is rhythmic. Give children an opportunity to experience rhythms.

Materials: several large balls; record or tape with a definite beat; record player or tape recorder

Directions: Depending on how many balls you have, let groups of children bounce the ball to the rhythm of the music. Turn off the music and have them stop and feel their pulses. Have them try to bounce the ball to the rhythm of their pulse.

Variation: Turn the music off. Have the children pretend to be their hearts. March, roll, or sway, to that special rhythm.

Materials: hand drum or can with sticks

Directions: Using the drum as the beat, instruct the children to march to the beat and/or bounce balls to the beat. Liken this to their heart beat.

Materials: drum; record or tape with strong beat

Directions: Have the children find a place in the room where they can not touch anyone. As the teacher calls out actions, the children move to the rhythm of the music using that action. For example, move forward, move up, or move down. Put your hands below your knees. Put your arms in back of you.

Valentine Chocolate Treats

Ingredients:

1 12 oz. (360 mL) package semisweet chocolate chips

1 cup (250 mL) plus 2 teaspoons (260 mL) evaporated milk, divided

3 cups (750 mL) fine vanilla wafer crumbs

2 cups (500 mL) miniature marshmallows

1 cup (250 mL) chopped walnuts

1 cup (250 mL) powdered sugar

Materials: pan and hot plate or microwave; square 8 or 9 inch (20 cm or 23 cm) pan; mixing spoons; spatula; measuring cup; one large mixing bowl and one small mixing bowl; knife

Directions: Put chocolate chips and 1 cup evaporated milk in a pan and melt in the microwave. Stir after 1 minute. Heat until chips are melted. In a large mixing bowl, combine crumbs, marshmallows, nuts, and powdered sugar. Reserve $\frac{1}{2}$ cup of the chocolate mixture for the glaze. Stir the remaining chocolate mixture into the crumb mixture. Blend well. Press evenly into a buttered 8 or 9 inch square pan.

For the glaze, stir in the remaining 2 teaspoons evaporated milk into the reserved $\frac{1}{2}$ cup chocolate mixture. Blend until the mixture is smooth. Spread evenly over the mixture in the pan. Chill until the glaze is set. Cut into squares. (Makes 32 small bars.)

Heart Healthy Recipes

Frozen Banana Sticks

Ingredients: Bananas (one banana for every 4 children); three lemons or lemon juice; popsicle sticks (one per child); knife; paper; pencil

Directions: If the book *Eating Fractions* by Bruce McMillan is available, read it to the children first to introduce fractions (See bibliography). Discuss dividing the banana in fourths. Give the children paper and pencils and let them draw a banana and divide it in four equal parts. Divide the class in groups of four and let each group make their own frozen banana sticks.

Directions for making the frozen banana stick: Peel the banana and cut it into fourths. Coat each piece with lemon juice and insert a popsicle stick in one end. Wrap the banana in freezer paper or sticky wrap. Freeze your new popsicle overnight and enjoy it the next day.

Variations: Try freezing apple slices, papaya slices, or kiwis and putting them on a stick. Dip the fruit in chopped nuts before you freeze it.

Frozen Fruit Cubes

Ingredients: thawed and prepared frozen fruit juice or canned fruit juice; popsicle sticks; ice cube trays

Directions: Pour juice into the ice cube trays. Place one popsicle stick in each cube of the tray. Freeze overnight. Enjoy the next day.

Variations:

- Place a strawberry, blueberry, etc. in the center of each cube and freeze with the juice. This makes a wonderful surprise for the children when they are licking their "juicesicle."

- Make the juice cubes without sticks and let the children enjoy them in a glass of water.

Valentine Bear Party

When you have finished studying about bears, have a Valentine Bear Party.

Materials: copies of the invitations (page 77); crayons or markers; scissors; red construction paper and glue (optional)

Directions: Decorate the bear invitations with crayons or markers. Cut hearts out of the red construction paper and glue on the bear, if desired. Turn the invitation over and fill in the blanks to invite parents to your party. Send this home about a week before the party.

Making Bear Name Tags

Materials: 5" x 8" (13 cm x 20 cm) note cards; yarn; hole punch; markers or crayons; pencils

Directions: Let the children find an acting partner and decide who will be Mr. Bear and Mrs. Bear. They will need to print Mr. or Mrs. Bear on the note card with pencil and then go over it with crayons or markers. Punch holes in the top and tie on yarn to make a necklace name tag.

Dramatization of the Book

Arrange the classroom so that groups of 6-8 parents will be seated together. The children will act out the play in front of the group where their parents are located. If parents need to change places to see their children, have them do this before the play begins.

Read *The Valentine Bears* to the guests. The children will need to decide ahead of time who will be Mrs. Bear and who will be Mr. Bear. Have them slip on the name tags and let the play begin!

Children love this type of activity and parents love seeing their child in a leading role. And since both roles are leading roles, everyone gets an opportunity to shine!

Valentine Chanting for Guests

Teacher Preparation: Write the poems that Mrs. Bear wrote for Mr. Bear on the chalkboard or on chart paper.

Directions: Have the children chant the poems in loud and soft voices for the guests. Ask the guests to join you. Try some of the variations for chants on page 67.

Play "You are Mine, You are Mine" on page 69 with the parents participating.

Sing "I Am Making Valentines" on page 70 and pass out special valentines to the guests.

Party Recipes

Fortune Cookies

Fortunes: Make the fortunes before starting to make the cookie recipe.

Materials: plain white paper cut into ½" x 2"/ 1.3 cm x 2.54 cm rectangles; felt tip markers

Directions: Have the children write a silly valentine message or fortune on each piece of paper. i. e. "Be my Balentine!" "Avoid heartburn," or "This is a covered ant!" Fold the message in half.

Cookies

Ingredients:

3 rolls of refrigerator sugar cookie dough
red sugar (for decorating the cookies)
cookie sheets
spatula
knife
papers with fortunes
written on them
waxed paper

Directions: Make the refrigerator cookies by following the directions given on the package. Slice them very thin. Fold the dough in half and slip the fortune inside. Seal the dough by pressing the edges together. Moisten the edge of the cookie with a dab of water to help the dough seal. Put the cookies on the cookie sheet, sprinkle them with red sugar and bake according to package instructions.

Valentine Deep Red Punch

Materials: punch bowl or large container; ladle; paper cups

Ingredients:

juice of 2 lemons
1 quart or 1 L grape juice
4 bottles of ginger ale, chilled

Add the lemon juice to the grape juice. Chill. Add ginger ale just before serving. Yield 24-30 servings.

Bulletin Board Ideas

Set the scene for a unit on Valentine's Day by creating a festive bulletin board.

Valentine Houses

Materials: red, white, or pink construction paper; heart patterns, page 13; house pattern, page 15; marker; stapler

Back the bulletin board with red, white, or pink paper. Using the three heart patterns on page 16, make enough small, medium, and large hearts to create a border of hearts. Reproduce as many houses as you wish on page 15. Color them. Choose a skill you wish to work on such as recognition of homonyms or addition facts. Label the house with a card underneath telling that specific skill. Write the word or problem on the windows and doors. Attach the houses onto the bulletin boards. Lift the flaps and write the answers underneath so that children may lift up the flaps to check their answers.

Student Created Displays

Using projects that students have made, create a bulletin board. Red, pink, or white paper can be used to back the bulletin board. Or use valentine wrapping paper to give it a special touch. Display childrens' work, such as the Pin Prick art on pages 65-66, or the Healthy Heart Collage on page 64. Give each child a heart to write his or her name on to put up next to his or her creation.

Letters to Parents

Dear Parents,

Your child is bringing home our class bear and bear journal today. The bear is his or her responsibility to take care of and return to school tomorrow. Your child may dress the bear, play with it, and add anything to the bag he or she would like the bear to have.

Please write or have your child write something the bear did with your child and/or your family in the journal. We will read it to the class tomorrow.

Return the bag with all its contents to school tomorrow. Another child is patiently waiting to take home our bear.

Thank you for your help.

Sincerely,

_____

Dear Parents,

We are starting a thematic unit on _____. Please send any books you might have on this subject. We also will need

_____

Be sure your child's name is on any items that he or she brings to school.

Thank you for your help in making this study meaningful to your child.

Sincerely,

_____

Letters to Parents *(cont.)*

Dear Parents,

Please come join us at our Valentine's Bear Party on

_____ at _____

We will have a "beary" good time!

Love,

_____

Dear Parents,

On _____, we will be celebrating Valentine's Day here at school. Your child can begin bringing Valentines on _____ or anytime after that.

Putting the valentines in the correct mailbox is an important reading activity. In order for your child to do this, please have your child sign his or her name on the card. Cut out the names on the attached class list and paste one name on each envelope.

Thank you for your help.

Happy Valentine's Day!

Sincerely,

_____

Valentine's Class List

Write one child's name in each box. Send home with the letter on page 77.

I,

have been studying about the heart and how to care for it.
Ask me what I know about the heart. I know a lot!

Presented by my teacher,

Teacher's Name

Date

Bibliography

Core Books

Bunting, Eve. *The Valentine Bears.* Houghton Mifflin, 1983
Bond, Felicia. *Four Valentines in a Rainstorm.* Harper Trophy, 1983
Sitts Graube, Ireta. *My Heart Book.* Teacher Created Materials, 1992

Fiction

Adams, Adrienne. *The Great Valentine's Day Balloon Race.* Charles Scribner's Sons, 1980
Brown, Marc. *Arthur's Valentine.* Little, Brown & Company, 1980
Cohen, Miriam. *Bee My Valentine!* Greenwillow, 1978
Devlin, Harry and Wende. *Cranberry Valentine.* Macmillan, 1986
Hoban, Lillian. *Arthur's Great Big Valentine.* Harper & Row, 1989
Hopkins, Lee Bennett. *Good Morning to You, Valentine.* HBJ, 1976
Hurd, Thacher. *Little Mouse's Big Valentine.* Harper & Row, 1990
Kelley, True. *A Valentine for Fuzzboom.* Houghton Mifflin, 1981
Mariana. *Miss Flora McFlimsey's Valentine.* Lothrop, Lee & Shepard, 1987
Modell, Frank. *One Zillion Valentines.* Greenwillow, 1981
Murphy, Shirley Rousseau. *Valentine For a Dragon.* Atheneum, 1984
Prelutsky, Jack. *It's Valentine's Day.* Greenwillow, 1983
Schulz, Charles M. *Be My Valentine, Charlie Brown.* Random House, 1976
Schweninger, Ann. *The Hunt For Rabbit's Galosh.* Doubleday, 1976
Schweninger, Ann. *Valentine Friends.* Puffin Books, 1988
Sharmat, Marjorie Weinman. *The Best Valentine In The World.* Holiday House, 1982
Smith, Janice Lee. *Nelson in Love.* Harper Collins, 1992
Stevenson, James. *Happy Valentine's Day, Emma!* Greenwillow, 1987
Stock, Catherine. *Secret Valentine.* Bradbury Press, 1991
Williams, Barbara. *A Valentine for Cousin Archie.* E.P. Dutton, 1981

Non-Fiction

Bright, Michael. *Polar Bear.* Gloucester Press, 1989
Bright, Michael. *Giant Panda.* Gloucester Press, 1989
Buxton, Jane. *Baby Bears & How They Grow.* National Geographic Society, 1986
Cole, Joanna. *The Magic School Bus Inside the Human Body.* Scholastic, 1989
Corwin, Judith Hoffman. *Valentine Fun.* Julian Messner, 1982
dePaola, Tomie. *Things to Make and Do for Valentine's Day.* Franklin Watts, 1976
Fradin, Dennis Brindell. *Valentine's Day.* Enslow Publishers, 1990
Glovach. Linda. *The Little Witch's Valentine Book.* Prentice-Hall, 1984
Kessel, Joyce K. *Valentine's Day.* Carolrhoda Books, 1981
LeMaster, Leslie Jean. *Your Heart and Blood.* Childrens Press, 1984
McMillan, Bruce. *Eating Fractions.* Scholastic, 1991
Newman, Pearl. *When Winter Comes.* Raintree, 1989
Parker, Steve. *The Heart and Blood.* Franklin Watts, 1989
Patent, Dorothy. *The Way of the Grizzly.* Clarion Books, 1987
Showers, Paul. *A Drop of Blood.* Thomas Y. Crowell, 1989
Showers, Paul. *You Can't Make a Move Without Your Muscles.* Thomas Y. Crowell, 1982
Showers, Paul. *Hear Your Heart.* Thomas Y. Crowell, 1968
Stone, Lynn. *Bears.* Rourke Corp., 1990
Supraner, Robyn. *Valentine's Day Things to Make and Do.* Troll Associates, 1981